Seeing My Time

Visual Tools for Executive Functioning Success

Instructor's Manual

By

Marydee Sklar

AGUANGA

Aguanga Publishing
Portland, Oregon

© 2010, 2012 Aguanga Publishing
6312 SW Capitol Hwy. Box 205
Portland, Oregon 97239-1938
www.ExecutiveFunctioningSuccess.com
First edition published 2010 under the title of *Seeing What I Need to Do—Instructor's Manual.*
Second edition 2012 published under the title of *Seeing My Time—Instructor's Manual.*

ISBN: 978-0-9826059-3-6
All rights reserved.

Thank you for honoring the author's tremendous number of hours and years that went into the development of these materials.

DEDICATION

In memory of my parents:

Mary Katherine Weiss
and
Dee Elmo Beattie

Their short lives taught me my life's greatest lesson—
the true value of time.

Contents

DEDICATION   iii

ACKNOWLEDGMENTS   vii

PREFACE TO THE SECOND EDITION   ix

INTRODUCTION   11

What You Need to Know   11
The Workbook—How to Use It   19
The *Course Notes*—How to Use Them   21
Course Format   25
Drawing to Back Up Words   27
Materials List   29

UNIT 1: THE BRAIN AND LEARNERS   31

Introduction: Setting the Stage
for *Seeing My Time*   31
Self-Reflection: Session #1 Check In   34
Little by Little, Change Happens   35
First Self-Assessments   37
Executive Skills   38
What I Need to Understand
About the Brain and Learners   44
More to Understand   58

UNIT 2: THE FIRST TRUTH OF TIME:
OUT OF SIGHT, OUT OF MIND   79

Out of Sight, Out of Mind   81
Tools for Time Management   84
Such Is Life . . .   93

UNIT 3: THE SECOND TRUTH OF TIME: TIME TAKES UP SPACE   95

Time Takes Up Space   98
Seeing What Takes Up
the Space of My Time   99
The Space in a Week   103
Summary of Weekly Planning   110
Whatever Needs to Get Done—
Be Sure to Keep It in Sight   112

UNIT 4: MEETING DUE DATES   113

Meeting Due Dates   114
Getting Projects Done on Time   115
Seeing My Assignment   116
Drawing My Assignment   118
Planning Backwards and Assigning Time   122
Planning the Time to Do the Steps   128
Getting It Done and Reaching Goals   131
To Get It Done—Just Start   132
Summary for Planning Ahead
by Planning Backwards   133

UNIT 5: ORGANIZATION AND PAPER MANAGEMENT   135

Organization and Paper Management   137
" . . . but I can't find it."   139
Handling Papers Away from Home   141
Handling Papers at Home   143
Creating a Useful Binder   146
The Planner: Your Best Friend—Use It   149
Papers Get Lost and Computers Die   152
Be Ready for Class or Meetings   153
The Brain Is *Not* Designed for Multitasking   155

UNIT 6: THE THIRD TRUTH OF TIME   157

The Way You Use Your Time Equals Your Life   159
Seeing My Future   161
Three Months of Goals   163
My Week of Actions   164
Summary for Reaching Goals   165

Changing My Behavior   166
Life Can Be Rough—You Gotta Be Tough   169
Second Self-Assessments   170
Plan Your Work—Work Your Plan   172

CHECK IN - CHECK OUT: 173
Self-Reflection: Session #1 Check Out   174
Self-Reflection: Session #2 Check In   176
Self-Reflection: Session #2 Check Out   177
Self-Reflection: Session #3 Check In   178
Self-Reflection: Session #3 Check Out   179
Self-Reflection: Session #4 Check In   180
Self-Reflection: Session #4 Check Out   181
Self-Reflection: Session #5 Check In   183
Self-Reflection: Session #5 Check Out   185
Self-Reflection: Session #6 Check In   186
Self-Reflection: Session #6 Check Out   187
Self-Reflection: Session #7 Check In   188
Self-Reflection: Session #7 Check Out   189
Nothing Changes if Nothing Changes   190
Self-Reflection: Sessions #8 and #9 Check In   192
Self-Reflection: Sessions #8 and #9 Check Out   193

APPENDIX   195
Session Record Form   196
Adult Self-Assessment Comparison   197
Student Self-Assessment Comparison   198
My Week of Actions   199
Week Sheet   200
Afternoon Sheet   201
My Day Sheet   202

BIBLIOGRAPHY   203

ABOUT THE AUTHOR   206

Acknowledgments

It is hard to write an original opening line for the acknowledgment section of a book. If you have written a book, you understand. If you have not, rest assured that the saying, "It takes a village to raise a child" can be adapted to say, "It takes a village to publish a book." I had no idea what I was going to learn when I started this project. It has been an adventure and would never have been possible without the encouragement, advice, skills, patience, support, and precious time of so many people. Working together, a dream has come true. Like having a child who has grown up in a community and left home, we send this work out into the world with great curiosity. It is our hope that the fruit of our efforts will be helpful to others.

I am full of gratitude for the following people: Dr. Jennifer Larsen for encouraging me to share my work. Dr. Ellyn Arwood for starting me on this path so many years ago by challenging me to think about my thinking. Carol Goss has been a supporter and believer in my work for years. Linda Hutchinson-Knowles, a perfect stranger met at a workshop of educational therapists, who took this introvert in tow and slogged through the first draft of this manual as she tested the program. Karen Marburger, who has so patiently read through the drafts and been a true friend and supporter when I hit a wall. Linda Hefferman appeared in my life exactly at the moment when I needed the expertise of a technical writer. She was key for helping me format a readable manual and gave me a hug when I really needed it. Marcia Hollander applied her wonderful concrete-sequential mind and editing skills to the manual to make sure that I was perfectly clear in what I wanted the instructor to do. Her insights and suggestions were a critical complement to my random-abstract brain. Jeff Fisher of Jeff Fisher Logomotives designed the cover. Ali McCart of Indigo Editing & Publications has applied her skillful eye to all the little details. Ed Kamholz of Designs by Design has been such a patient mentor and partner in turning my documents into a book. Charlie Clark of Charlie Clark Books has handled all the printing details, creating a book lovely to hold.

When you are writing a book to deadline, so much of your normal life goes on hold. It takes a very special family to understand. First, thanks to my sister and brother-in-law, Sandra and Robert

Redding. They let me stay in their cabin to write the first draft, providing dinner and wood for the wood stove. While technically not family, I couldn't have kept up my home-based practice and also written the book without Veronica Castillo keeping the house clean each week. My son, Josh, solved all my computer issues and kept telling me, "You can do it, Mom." His own determination has sustained mine. Kat Wilson not only manages my bookkeeping but helped me create a wonderful office space to work in, including putting together a very complicated desk. My daughter, Katie, has always given excellent advice and is an encouraging cheerleader. She lives her life fully, inspiring me to do the same. Finally, I could not have done this without the support of my dear husband of twenty-eight years, Ron Sklar. He has stepped in and taken over running the household, making sure that I've been well fed. He is so appreciated. We make a good team.

My appreciation also goes to all of my clients who have shared their challenges and successes.

Thank you all for being part of an exciting journey.

Preface to the Third Edition

The hardest part of writing a book is stopping. There is always one more idea, one more change, one more edit. When you finally hold the book in your hands you inevitably find errors and think of ways to make it better.

This third edition cleans up a few errors and adds a few new tips. It also reflects a reorganization made in the companion *Seeing My Time* workbook.

The most obvious change is in the title. The previous title, *Seeing What I Need to Do,* was just too long, so like the *Course Notes*, the main title has been shortened to *Seeing My Time.* This third edition also introduces The Sklar Process®—Much More Than Time Management. This phrase is now used to describe my whole program.

Introduction

What You Need to Know

The Sklar Process is a program designed for professionals to use with their clients, students or employees who are struggling and failing because of deficits in the executive functioning skills of time management and organization.

The program consists of this *Instructor's Manual* which is to be used with the six-unit *Seeing My Time* workbook that students or clients complete with your guidance.

The program covers the following:

- Executive functioning skills of the brain

- Background knowledge about the connection between the brain and behavior

- How and why to use effective external tools to compensate for what the brain can't do

- How and why to plan your week and your day using visual external strategies

- How to break a complex project into steps using visual strategies

- How to plan the time to work on parts of a project in order to meet a deadline

Definition

In the context of this book, **executive functioning skills** refer to those processes in the brain that control our behavior and enable us to get things done effectively and efficiently. In essence, I am talking about time-management and organization skills. These executive functioning skills are located primarily in the prefrontal cortex of the brain.

- How to manage paper and create a personal binder/planner

- How to prepare for class or meetings

- How to begin working on future goals and dreams

- How to be realistic about the process of changing behavior and developing efficient time-management skills

Client Profile

This program is appropriate to use with individuals from middle schoolers through adults who present with the following issues:

- Poor time management

- Procrastination connected to starting work or projects

- Failure to meet deadlines

- Failure to plan ahead

- Over-scheduling

- Poor paper management

Adults can be taught one-on-one or in groups. For maximum effectiveness, adolescents should take the course in the company of at least one parent, although having both parents is ideal. Individual family groups can meet with the instructor, or the course can be offered to groups of parents and their children, grades 5–12.

About This Program

The *Seeing My Time Instructor's Manual* that you are holding in your hands is the result of answering three questions. I asked myself the first question almost eighteen years ago: **how do you support a brain that has no awareness of time?** I was motivated to find the answer because of a bright, frustrated woman suffering from low self-esteem and producing well below her potential. That woman was me.

When I started my quest, I felt very alone—living with a self-imposed label of an underachieving procrastinator. At the time, people weren't talking about the brain and executive functioning deficits as the source of challenges with time management.

Definition

I believe that I was the first to use the term **time-challenged**. I use it to describe a person who has time-management issues: trouble meeting deadlines, often late for appointments or work, forgets appointments, etc. I came up with it because, as a person who is only five feet tall, I've joked about being vertically challenged for years, unable to reach items from cupboards and shelves in grocery stores.

Tip

I make comparisons between being vertically challenged and being time-challenged. As a short person, I have four possible responses to being unable to reach something on a shelf:

1. I can give up and not get it.

2. I can rant and rave about how unfair it is that people makes shelves so high.

3. I can ask for help.

4. I can use a tool to help me, like a step stool.

The time-challenged have the same four options. I encourage my clients to do the last two: ask for help or use a tool to support their brain.

Thankfully, a professor ahead of the pack, Dr. Ellyn Arwood at the University of Portland, challenged me to use my visual thinking to solve my issues with time management. She gave me the obscure advice to "go home and take care of yourself in time and space and come back to see me." It took me a year to figure out what she meant. At the end of that time, my life was on a different course. I knew what I had to do to support my brain, and why. I finally knew how to get things done on time and feel in control of my days for the first time in over forty years.

In my work as an educator helping children with learning challenges, it became obvious that I was not the only person who had a brain that was time-challenged. Everywhere I looked I saw bright children struggling and failing in school because of incomplete work and missing assignments. Often at least one of their parents had similar time and organization issues. They were all so frustrated and in such painful conflict with each other.

Now I had a second question to answer: **can I transmit my insights about the brain and time to others—adolescents and adults?**

The short answer: yes.

As an educator with a passion for learning and teaching, I've now spent years with families and individuals analyzing their challenges and refining my program. Without intending it, I've become known by professionals in my community as a specialist in executive functioning.

This took about fourteen years of working with people and tinkering with the methods and materials. I've become good at teaching time management to families and adults, and soon professionals in my circle were encouraging me to publish my work. This was very flattering, but I had my doubts. Was my success based upon the program I had developed or upon the force of my personality, my gifts as a teacher, my many years of experience?

This led to the third question: **are others coming to the same conclusions about what is needed to teach time management as I am?**

The short answer: yes.

You see, while I was focusing on the needs of the people who came to me, researchers in neuroscience and neuropsychology across the country were also focusing on the bright children and adults who were struggling and failing because they couldn't seem to sustain production: to get things done on time.

Executive functioning is the phrase used to describe the processes in the brain that are, in part, connected to getting things done on time: our ability to produce, our time management. It has been a key topic on the speaker's podium for many professional conferences. Everyone working with bright, failing students, and those with ADHD, is looking for answers for their struggling clients. Relatively unknown just a few years ago, executive functioning is now the topic for books that are being produced to meet the need for more information. The concept of executive functioning has filtered down from academia to professionals, and now to parents, as more and more children are being evaluated and diagnosed with deficits in executive functioning.

Developing Metacognition Is Key

My third question—**are others on the same track as me?**—started getting answers when I flew to Berkeley to attend a workshop sponsored by the Association of Educational Therapists (AET). Dr. Charles Ahern, of the Watershed Learning Institute, was presenting "Executive Functioning and Learning." He is a professor, neuropsychologist, and educational therapist with a private practice helping learners one-on-one. As he spoke, my mind raced, making connections between his work and my own. It was very exciting as I sat in the audience, my latest version of my workbook on my lap, under my notes. When an educational therapist raised her hand and asked, "But how exactly do I teach this?" I thought: "I know how. It's right here in my lap."

Ahern, and others, including Lynn Meltzer, author of *Promoting Executive Function in the Classroom*, have found that the ability to reflect upon your learning and behavior is a critical component in developing the self-awareness required to actually use effective strategies to support a time-challenged brain. With increased metacognition—thinking about your thinking—comes behavior change.

After his talk, I had just one question for Dr. Ahern. When my turn came, I asked, "So, does it all boil down to metacognition?" His answer was the briefest I've ever gotten from a professor:

"Yes."

Definition

Metacognition is a fancy way of saying "thinking about your thinking."

Fostering metacognition is one foundation for the success of *Seeing My Time.* The time-challenged are unconscious of the passage of time. Metacognition brings time into consciousness. One of my adult clients said that for him, developing metacognition connected to time meant that he now had a second voice track in his mind. He was now pausing to listen to this second track that was telling him things like, "Is this what I need to be focusing on?" or, "It's time to stop and start the next task on the list."

As I developed *The Sklar Process,* I intuitively saw the need for participants to have the time to pause and reflect as the course progressed. As a result there are many pages in the workbook dedicated to developing metacognition.

External Strategies Support the Brain

It was another trip to California that helped me understand a second reason my program works. At the 2009 national conference of AET, Dr. Russell Barkley, renowned for his research connected to ADHD, provided a full-day presentation titled, "The Link Between ADHD, Self-Regulation, and Executive Functioning."

Once again, my brain was whirring as I found ties between his comments and my work. Barkley gave me a key word and concept that applies to *Seeing My Time.* In a nutshell, he told us that if the brain can't do it, then a person has to use external support strategies. Time management has to be externalized.

I had long been teaching this to my clients under the guise of the old expression: "Out of sight, out of mind." I explain that the nature of time itself makes time management difficult. It is an abstract concept that is invisible. We can't see time. The solution is to use tools to make time concrete and visible.

The strategies taught in *Seeing My Time* are all about externalizing time management. Tools are used to keep time in sight and thus in mind.

Use Visual Hands-On Methods

The third foundation for the success of my program is its visual, hands-on method of instruction. Years ago when Ellyn Arwood identified me as a visual thinker, it was a rather radical idea. Today the vast majority of the time-challenged adolescents and adults I've worked with readily self-identify as visual learners: benefiting from seeing what they need to learn versus only hearing what

---

Resource

Russell Barkley has created executive functioning assessments scales for both adults and children (2011, 2012). He has also written a thorough book on the topic: *Executive Functions—What They Are, How They Work, and Why They Evolved* which outlines his model. All are listed in the bibliography.

Key Point

We can't see time. The solution is to use tools to make time concrete and visible.

they need to learn. Researchers like Lynn Meltzer encourage using visual strategies to teach individuals with executive functioning deficits.

Based on my own brain and experience, I designed *The Sklar Process* to focus on using the strengths of the visual learner. The instructor is directed to back up lecturing with hand-drawn visuals on a dry erase board. The course participants are encouraged to draw their responses to the reflection questions rather than write sentences. The activities that make time concrete and visual engage the visual and kinesthetic learning modalities by including drawing combined with sticky notes and flags.

Provide Clients Knowledge about the Brain

The fourth reason this program works is because in the first unit, I never talk about time management. I never mention strategies. Instead of focusing on behavior, I focus on the brain. I give the participants critical background knowledge about metacognition (yes, I use that word right off the bat), executive functioning skills, brain development, learning strengths, what is happening in the brain as we learn, the emotional responses to unsuccessful learning, and how it affects our behavior. I draw about how schools are designed for one kind of brain and how the business world is looking for the skills of other kinds of brains. I discuss why successful learners have to be honest and have courage. And I provide a visual analogy to set up a discussion about motivation and the choices we have as learners: to work hard, to slack off, or to give up.

I began starting my course this way after reading *A Mind at a Time* by pediatrician and learning specialist Mel Levine. He used the term *demystification* to describe the process of helping children understand themselves and what they have to work on. Like Levine, I have found that giving participants knowledge about the biological basis of their time challenges is very freeing. Suddenly they are not bad and lazy—for the time-challenged are walking wounded. In the first hour, some of the guilt and shame slips away. Their pain has been acknowledged. They leave the first session with a glimmer that there is hope for them yet. It is this hope that creates the buy-in to the program, to actually using the strategies. This is especially necessary for the adolescent client.

Add Magic to Your Sessions

And finally, if there is any personal magic to my sessions, it's my enthusiasm and my ability to show compassion for my clients. I create a safe place to learn by having fun with them. I tell people at the first session that I want to work with them only if I'm going to have fun doing it. (I love watching the faces of teens when I say that.) I share my own executive functioning weaknesses. I share my amazement at my successes and changes. I am honest with them about how hard it is to change behavior. I use humor whenever possible.

I am rarely sitting down yak-yaking at them. Instead I'm up drawing on the dry erase board or dramatizing a story or moving around the table, giving each participant personal attention and encouragement. I give them stretch breaks. Those who need to, can stand while they fill in the workbook. Most of all, as I've been told, I am enthusiastic. I truly believe—know—that they can improve their time-management behaviors, and my enthusiasm and optimism rubs off on them.

You Too Can Be an Effective Teacher

The focus of this work is to provide you with the essential knowledge needed to effectively teach time management. Critical concepts and information have been distilled into a carefully scaffolded program accessible to both adolescents and adults.

As I built my program, I attended conferences, courses, and workshops, and I read, searching out wisdom to help me reach and teach my clients. Throughout the manual I acknowledge those who provided pivotal bits of information or perspectives which I have found useful. It is beyond the scope of this work to provide extensive background information about executive functioning. For that, I refer you to excellent sources listed in the bibliography at the end of this book.

My contribution, the *Seeing My Time* program, is unique because I am a rare bird. I understand the issues from the inside, and I am an experienced teacher, understanding the needs of learners in a learning process. You too will be a learner as you go through this manual. I designed it to support you, step-by-step, to develop the skills to teach time management to the time-challenged.

You Don't Have to Be Time-Challenged

An educator friend wondered if she would be an effective teacher of the course because she has a time-based brain, unlike mine. I assured her that the workbook and *Instructor's Manual* are designed to support a variety of instructors as well as clients.

For anyone who picks up this manual, it is going to be a learning experience to instruct the course for the first couple of times. Since the workbook and *The Sklar Process* are designed specifically to appeal to—and meet the needs of—the time-challenged, your clients will quickly be comfortable with the materials and methods.

So, plunge in to help your clients. Follow the manual. Just looking at the pages in the workbook will provide support. Over time, you'll be tweaking the program here and there, adding your own stories. Have fun with it. There is joy in mastering new material outside of your comfort zone.

You can do this!

Begin at the Beginning

I invite you to begin at the beginning of the manual and pause and respond to all the questions, drawing answers when asked. Work through Unit 1, and then invite someone to be your client and guide them through the process. You only have to be one unit ahead of them.

The manual supplies a minimal script. Use it as the framework for your own stories and observations. Just cover the key talking points for each section, and your clients will bloom before your eyes. I've added some stories for more background as well as lots of visual examples.

The companion book, the *Seeing My Time* workbook, provides a place for your clients to record their learning and becomes a permanent resource for them to sustain their time-management skills. It is available at my website: www.ExecutiveFunctioningSuccess.com. My clients treasure their workbook as a resource to sustain their time-management behavior changes and yours will too.

Teaching adolescents and adults how to develop time-management skills is very rewarding. I have fun teaching the course and changing lives as I teach critical life skills. You too can make a dramatic difference in the lives of your struggling time-challenged clients. Give them knowledge. Give them tools. Give them hope!

Enjoy *Seeing My Time* and feel free to contact me through my website at www.ExecutiveFunctioningSuccess.com. I'd love to hear about your experience using the program. I'm always looking for ways to improve it.

Marydee Sklar

Tip

Fill In your own copy of the workbook, doing the activities as you read about them in the manual. This practice experience will help you see and understand how the program works. (You might even improve your own time management in the process.) In the future, as you work with clients, you can refer to your workbook. Since a picture is worth a thousand words, your workbook will easily support you as you instruct. And, in the margins, you can make notes to yourself about key points to cover.

While I instruct, my copy of the workbook is in front of me so I can match the participants' work page-by-page.

This *Instructor's Manual*— How to Use It

First, be sure to read the *Instructor's Manual* up to the beginning of Unit 1: The Brain and Learners. This is where it connects to the *Seeing My Time* workbook used by participants, and the first session of *The Sklar Process*. The introduction pages provide you:

- Background about the program

- How to use the *Seeing My Time* workbook.

- An outline of the course format

- Advice about drawing

- A list of materials you will need to conduct the course

This manual will guide you, step-by-step, as you and your clients progress through the workbook, page-by-page.

For each page in the *Seeing My Time* workbook, the *Instructor's Manual* provides the following:

- Background information on the page topic

- What you need to do and say:

  Under the subheading **What I Do**, you will find talking points and occasionally a script for what to say. If appropriate, there will also be an illustration showing you what to draw on a dry erase board to back up your lecture, or a sample illustration of what a completed form might look like.

- Directions for the client activity:

  Under the subheading **Activity**, you will find specific directions for the participants, which allows them to complete the page in the workbook.

In the sidebars you will find a selection of stories, tips, and key points to support your teaching. The appendix includes forms to copy for use in sessions as well as a bibliography of recommended reading.

To begin, I suggest you read the introduction to the *Instructor's Manual* and then skim through the workbook. Then I'd set aside some time to go through Unit 1, reading the manual and doing the activities. At that point you are ready to teach! You only need to be one unit ahead of your clients. Go for it. You can do it.

Tip

How to pace sessions to complete the workbook in a given number of sessions is turning out to be the biggest challenge for new instructors leading folks through the *Seeing My Time* workbook.

I tell new clients upfront that people usually complete the six units of the program in around eight sessions, some less, some more. I leave it open-ended and charge by the session.

The *Seeing My Time* Workbook— How to Use It

Going cover-to-cover through the *Seeing My Time* workbook is central to the success of *The Sklar Process*. It provides the participants with a structure that builds understanding and the hands-on experience required to develop the executive skills of time management and paper organization. The workbook was designed to be a long-lasting reference book and tool, useful after the completion of the course. It contains forms, which the participants have permission to reproduce for their own use.

Six Units of Study

The program is broken into six units of study:

Unit 1: The Brain and Learners
Unit 2: The First Truth of Time—Out of Sight, Out of Mind
Unit 3: The Second Truth of Time—Time Takes Up Space
Unit 4: Meeting Due Dates—Planning Ahead by Planning Backwards
Unit 5: Organization and Paper Management
Unit 6: The Third Truth of Time—The Way You Use Your Time Equals Your Life

Session Length, Number, and Audience

Generally speaking, it takes me seven to nine hours of client time to complete the course with an adolescent and a parent. I have done this for so long that I power through the material at a fairly rapid pace. For instructors new to presenting the course, I suggest you tell families to plan on seven to nine sessions to complete the program. Over time, you will get a feel for how you want to pace the sessions. It will also vary depending on the participants.

Sometimes participants arrive with a crisis situation at school or work that requires your support. In these circumstances I tell the participants that they have a choice. Time can be taken out of the course to work on the problem at hand. However, they would have to add another session to complete the course material. So far, all my clients have opted to add a session.

Since it may take as many as seven to nine sessions to cover six units, there is not a direct correlation between the concept of a session and a unit. Each session has its own beginning and ending activity (Check In and Check Out), all unit activities may not fit neatly into one specific session. This means that some unit content will spill over into the next session.

I have presented the course in the following session formats to accommodate a variety of audiences:

Weekly: I meet with participants once a week, for sixty minutes. This works with both individual adults and students with a parent. In many ways this is the preferred format because it allows time between sessions to practice strategies.

Intensive: In the three weeks prior to school starting, I will meet with students and a parent for five days in a row, for sixty-minute sessions. The final sessions are scheduled for after the start of school.

While not ideal for maximum learning, this is very popular because many teens have demanding academic schedules and extracurricular activities that make it difficult to schedule weekly meetings after school starts. (From a business point of view, the intensive program means I work with five to six families a day.)

Ninety-Minute Sessions: In some cases it works to meet in longer sessions with adults and older high school and college students. This enables them to fit the course into their work or school schedules.

Ninety-Minute Group Sessions: I have met with students and parents for evening or Saturday programs that are ninety-minute long sessions. With this format the program is completed over the span of seven meetings.

Single Two-Hour Group Session: I once presented a shortened version of the program, focusing on time-management basics, to a group of over twenty-five women just out of prison and on parole.

I estimate that the average reading level for those women was about third grade. Since the *Seeing My Time* materials emphasize drawing answers versus writing them, it was a user-friendly program for them. It was a very enlightening experience for both the women and me. Because of my program, they received watches, clocks, and planners—tools they desperately needed to function in work settings.

Tip

If you are a tutor or an educational therapist meeting weekly during the school year with a student to provide academic support, it is challenging to present this program while also helping with homework. Properly done, this course requires sessions dedicated exclusively to the program material. I've tried to do both, and both suffer.

My solution is to offer *The Sklar Process* as a separate service, done in addition to tutoring sessions. That said, an educational therapist who was testing the program with a client took, for various reasons, over five months to complete the program. While this would not be recommended, the family did report value in the course.

Classrooms: I was once invited to present the course to a class of fifth-graders at the very end of the school year, to prepare them for the transition to middle school. Over four days I gave them the time-management basics and binder organization. The students loved it. The teacher loved it. Before I left the building, they hired me to come back the next fall.

However, we learned something very important that September. Developmentally, incoming fifth-graders, unlike graduating fifth-graders, were not ready for an intense course in time management. The teacher and I decided for that age group, it would have been better to introduce the program in bits over time, with lots of teacher support for practice. We would have started with paper management and then moved on to the activities that teach time concepts and strategies.

It would be easy to use the *Seeing My Time* workbooks in middle and high school classrooms. To be most effective, the teacher would want to also have a parent-night class to explain how to use the tools and strategies. Parents should be included because they need to support the development of their children's time-management skills.

It's OK to Be Flexible

Seeing My Time is carefully organized and structured to support learning and behavior change. That said, you might end up wanting to change the order of how you present the units.

From my experience it is very important to always begin with Unit 1 and Unit 2 before introducing any of the other units. They provide critical information that your clients need in order to understand the remaining units. (Trust me. You don't save time by leaving them out.)

One unit that can move around is Unit 5: Organization and Paper Management. If you are working during the school year with a student who is really struggling because of missing papers and assignments, then it might be wise to spend time on binder organization before going to time management, which begins in Unit 3. When I've been confronted with a reluctant or resistant teen, I have sometimes jumped ahead to the final unit: The Third Truth of Time—The Way You Use Your Time Equals Your Life. I'll do just the initial activities of the unit: drawing their future, to help them get out of their present conflicts and resistance to look ahead to their future. Picturing their dreams and hopes can help them consider the possibility that the course will help them.

The Forms Are Starting Points

One of the joys of teaching this program is that the time-challenged tend to be creative, out-of-the-box thinkers. As we go through the course, using the forms I've designed, I always let them know that they are free to come up with their own adaptation of my ideas. The important thing is for them to understand the need to use external tools to support their brain. I'm always thrilled when students come back to a session and report that they made their own form or found some other tool that is useful for them. When they are coming up with their own solutions, they are successfully applying course concepts. When they are feeling successful, I know that I've been successful.

Course Format

Each session has four components: a brief review, a check-in for self-reflection, a series of activity pages, and a check-out for self-reflection. The four components are described in detail below.

In the workbook, the self-reflection pages are located at the back of the book, beginning on page 65. In this *Instructor's Manual* you will find the directions for the check-in and check-out pages beginning on page 173. Since these directions do not follow in line with the unit material, I suggest you flag the section for quick access during your sessions.

Check In

•Review:

For effective learning of the course content, allow participants quiet time to silently review the material they have been covering since the beginning of the course. Repeated exposure is a critical component in creating learning and behavior change.

•Self-Reflection:

The check-in points correspond to sitting down for a session. They do not necessarily correspond to beginning a unit of the course, since some units will flow into the following session.

Have everyone respond to the check-in prompts at the beginning of each session. Then have participants share their answers.

This check-in time is a key component for developing metacognition connected to time management. It is also an opportunity to discuss problems and provide guidance for personalized problem-solving strategies.

What I Do

The manual you are reading now provides explanations of what you should do in relation to each page in the workbook and, when appropriate, gives you an example of how to draw to support your lecture.

Activity

•Allow time for the participants to complete the activities. Some pages go faster than others. Watch the clock and pace the session

---

Useful Quote

"Repeat to remember ... remember to repeat."
John Medina in *Brain Rules*

Tip

It is important not to take sides if the participants arrive at the session in a state of conflict over time-management issues. Stay positive and act as a mediator. Be careful not to let either child or parent dominate. Good luck.

so you don't spend too much time discussing the simpler pages.

- **Leave your drawings on the board** until the clients have completed the activity in their workbook.

- **Allow participants time to briefly share their responses to each activity** and give them feedback as necessary. This is especially important for family groups. Parents get a window into the minds of their adolescent, and the child gets to see the adult being less than perfect as they share their own challenges with time management.

Check Out

Give participants a couple minutes at the end of the session to answer the prompts.

- **Key Idea:**

  This is the take-home idea or concept from the session that had the greatest value for the participant.

- **A Strategy to Try:**

  Units 2–6 all provide external strategies that participants may choose to use.

- **Assignment:**

  The *Instructor's Manual* will provide the assignment for the first three sessions. Subsequent sessions allow participants to decide their own assignment, which encourages them to take ownership of using the strategies.

Tip

In families where a parent is as time-challenged as the child, sharing can open up the opportunity to have a conversation about how child and parent can support each other to develop better time-management skills. Mutual support removes the adversarial role of the parent.

Drawing to Back Up Words

Resources:

If you need help visualizing how to draw ideas, check out these two books:

Mapping Inner Space: Learning and Teaching Visual Mapping by Nancy Margulies

The Back of the Napkin: Solving Problems and Selling Ideas with Pictures by Dan Roam

Tip

Dan Roam, author of *The Back of the Napkin*, calms people's fear of drawing by asking them to do the following:

1. Draw a circle.

2. Draw a square.

3. Draw an arrow that connects the circle and the square.

4. Draw a stick figure.

5. For extra credit, put a smiley face on your stick figure.

If you can do those five things, you have the necessary drawing skills required to follow the directions in this manual.

Pictures Help Visual Thinkers Learn

A lot of people freeze up when I ask them to draw their ideas. They immediately think, "I'm not an artist. I can't do that." If you are one of those people, please take a deep breath and read on. You are not alone.

I gave a presentation on *Seeing My Time* to speech pathologists at a state conference. At a discussion point, one raised her hand and said, "When you started the presentation and told me that I was supposed to draw my notes, I almost left because I don't draw. My mind doesn't work that way. But now I realize that my students *need* me to draw because that's how their minds work. It's not about me and what I like." When she shared this, I wanted to jump up and down. Changing that one woman's point of view about drawing to support her students' learning made the six hours of driving for that conference worthwhile.

You Don't Have to Be an Artist

I am responsible for the drawings in this manual, and you will readily see that I am not an artist. I could have hired an illustrator or one of my talented students to do the drawings, but I wanted you to see how I actually do it on my dry erase board. This kind of drawing is more along the lines of symbolic icons rather than representational art.

Before I start to draw, I tell my clients that it is going to be painfully apparent that I am not an artist. I don't expect them to be artists. I use drawings because it is true that a picture is worth a thousand words. The first thing I draw is a brain, and I sometimes ask them to guess what it is. People have guessed a coffee bean or a walnut. The best part about not being an artist is that I'm so bad that almost all of my clients immediately think, "I can do better than that." And they can! You will be amazed at what they produce when they represent their ideas in pictures.

Drawing Helps Visual Thinkers Remember

Encouraging visual thinkers to draw their notes is novel for them and ultimately very useful. They can scan a picture very quickly and remember the lecture details more easily than scanning a page of words. Ellyn Arwood explained to me that being a visual thinker is a little bit like being bilingual because you are constantly translating in your head, taking the words you hear and turning them into pictures and vice versa. It's more effective and efficient to just skip the word notes and go to the pictures. (It took me a while to break the word notes habit even though they were not useful—I never reread them. Now I create very useful notes which are a combination of drawings and words.) After discussing the value of his visual notes in the workbook, a twenty-year-old student asked, "Can I take notes like this in class?" When I said, "Of course," his eyes lit up, a big smile came over his face, and he said, "All right!"

Materials List

This is a master list of all materials required for conducting the *Seeing My Time* course. Materials needed are also listed at the beginning of each unit and activity.

Units 1 through 6 will always need the following items:

- Dry erase board, markers, and eraser

- For each participant (parents included) a copy of the *Seeing My Time* workbook

- Sharp pencils with erasers

- 3 x 5 cards

Unit 1

- Self-Assessment Comparison form for each participant (See the appendix)

Unit 2

- Small analog clock

- Small digital clock

- Digital timers

- Sample two-page Month Calendar

- A My Day Sheet (See the appendix)

- A Week Sheet (See the appendix)

- Any size box with a lid

Unit 3

- Sticky arrow flags

- Week Sheet (In the appendix)

Tip

I hate shopping for specific items. Stores keep low inventory and change what they stock.

To help instructors and course participants, I put a Cool Tools page on my website. You will be able to find links to:
- A small analog clock
- Sticky arrow flags
- Two-pocket transparent plastic pocket folders
- Two-pcket plastic pocket dividers
- Easy-access sheet protectors

I've also included links to books I've found useful. Check out www.Executive FunctioningSuccess.com

•Afternoon Week Sheet (In the appendix)

•My Day Sheet (In the appendix)

•Plastic sheet protector

•Optional: Two sample posters of children's and adults' roles

Unit 4

•Highlighter marker for each participant

•Pads of the smallest sticky notes: approximately 2″ x 1 1/2″

•Optional: Foil stars

Unit 5

•A timer with a count-up function

•A two-pocket transparent plastic folder

•Two-pocket insertable plastic pocket dividers

•Easy-access sheet protectors

•Two-page Month Calendar

Unit 6

•Self-Assessment Comparison form (In the appendix)

Unit 1:
The Brain
and Learners

Introduction—Setting the Stage for *Seeing My Time*

There is no magic wand to solve time-management challenges that are based in executive functioning deficits. By explaining about the brain–behavior connection you depersonalize the guilt and blame that has been haunting time-challenged people for years. They aren't bad or lazy people. It is the wiring in their brain that has been the source of the problem, not personal will.

Tears Can Flow

It is not uncommon to have emotional outbursts in sessions, usually tears. I once had a failing ninth-grader burst into tears within the first four minutes of meeting her. All I'd done was introduce myself and tell a little bit about the course. When I asked her what was happening for her, she replied, "I can't believe that I'm such a bad person that I have to be here." By the end of the session, she walked out smiling and visibly lighter. She wasn't bad. She now understood that her brain's wiring was behind her challenges. She left feeling hopeful that change was possible.

Begin with the Brain

In the first unit of *Seeing My Time*, time management is not the topic. That will come in Unit 2. Instead, this first unit and session is about connecting. You will be connecting to your clients and they to you. You will be giving them information that they will be able to connect to their own behavior.

You will be focusing not on your client's behavior, but on information about their brain and its connection to behavior. It is very important to start with this focus because your time-challenged

Key Points

1. The time-challenged experience emotional pain connected to their struggles with getting things done on time.

2. It takes courage for them to come to the first session of the course.

3. Focus on teaching about the brain and not on your client's past behavior.

4. It takes time and patience to build time-management skills.

clients are emotionally very vulnerable. They can be very defensive. To have arrived in your office, they have a long and painful history of failure connected to time management. Adolescents and young adults are particularly wary and reluctant to be there. Adults with ADHD may be looking for help, but are fearful of failing again—fearful of even having hope that they can improve their lives.

By not making the clients' behavior the focus, you give them room to relax. Somewhere in the first session, there is information that will strongly connect to your client. It varies from person to person. When they make that connection ("I've felt that way" or "I've done that" or "That explains it") they have bought into the course, letting down their defenses. They see possibilities for change if they stay. They have hope that they can be productive without all the stress, drama, and conflict they have been experiencing.

As an instructor you need to be gentle, encouraging, and completely honest. By honest, I mean being upfront with your clients. There is no magic wand to solve their problems. This is a process. It takes time. It takes commitment.

You also have to be honest when you are faced with a client who is dedicated to being resistant to the whole program, unwilling to buy in and do the work. When I have these clients (they are rare, but they do show up), I tell them that we are not a match. Since I am not a counselor or therapist who deals with deeply rooted resistant emotional behaviors, I send them home, with a referral if they are willing to take it. I won't waste my time, their time, or their money. I tell them to give me a call if they ever decide that they would like my help in the future. Some have come back, years later!

Beyond connecting to your clients, the purpose of this unit is to give the participants background knowledge about the brain, learning, and behavior. In the process you are creating a common vocabulary and introducing ideas and concepts that you will refer back to as the program progresses.

Some teens are initially resistant to participating in the course. This is normal. Engaging them requires sharing some of your own vulnerability, being honest with them, and using humor whenever possible. And don't outright take sides with the parent. Stay neutral. However, sit closest to the teen and focus most of your attention on him or her.

MATERIALS NEEDED:

- Dry erase board, markers, and eraser
- For each participant (parents included) a copy of the *Seeing My Time* workbook
- Sharp pencils with erasers
- 3 x 5 cards

WHAT I DO:

1. **Introduce** yourself to the participants, welcoming them.

2. **Pass out** copies of the workbook and have participants write their name on the line below the word *by* on the title page. Since participants will be adding illustrations and comments to the workbook it is appropriate that they be co-authors.

3. **Point out** that they will be producing a work that they will be able to keep for future reference.

4. **Direct** participants to page 9.

Page 9:
Self-Reflection
Session #1 Check In

I usually begin the check-in process by asking participants if they have ever been white-water rafting. If they haven't, I ask if they could imagine what it would be like. I explain that if they never develop good time-management skills, then their life is going to feel like going down a white-water river without any paddles. It is not a pretty sight. They'll have little control. Completing the *Seeing My Time* workbook—cover-to-cover—will allow them to develop both the understanding and strategies needed to solve their time-management challenges. They'll have the paddles needed to direct their life.

WHAT I DO:

1. **Ask** participants to answer the check-in prompt.

2. **Allow** a brief bit of time for everyone to read their answers.

3. **Provide** a brief description of the program:

   • One goal of the course is to help people lower their stress and conflicts caused by poor time-management skills.

   • Another goal is to help people to manage their time so they can get quality work done on deadline.

   • The program was designed by an educator who is herself time-challenged. She struggled for years, not meeting her potential, until she figured out her brain was the source of her time-management problems. This course comes from her success at helping first herself and then many others.

   • There will be seven to nine sessions. Each session will focus on different topics and strategies needed to effectively manage time.

   • The workbook is designed especially for the creative, visual thinker. Participants will be encouraged to draw their notes.

   • It'll be fun!

Tip

As you begin to draw on the dry erase board, it is the first place both to use humor and to expose your own imperfection, especially if you don't think of yourself as an artist. Laugh at your drawings. In fact, if you are pretty awful, it gives the participants confidence that they can do better than you!

Page 10:
Little by Little, Change Happens

I emphasize the point that there is no magic wand to fix the participants' time-management struggles by having a pencil in my hand pretending it is a magic wand. As I wave my "wand," I look them in the eye and tell them that I really wish I did have a magic wand because it hurts to see all the pain in the world that is caused by poor time-management skills. I joke that if I had such a magic wand, I'd first fund my retirement, and then I'd run around giving away my magic.

WHAT I DO:

1. **Direct** participants to page 10.

2. **Ask** a participant to read aloud the words: *Little by little, change happens.*

3. **Discuss** what those words mean, including the following points:

    •There is no magic wand to fix their time-management problems.

    •It is a step-by-step process to develop the skills and strategies necessary to use time well in order to get things done.

    •There is no quick fix. It is critically important to be honest and up front with everyone at the table on this point.

4. **Explain** that in this course, everyone is encouraged to take notes and answer questions with drawings instead of traditional sentences. It might take a little getting used to, but give it a try.

5. On the dry erase board, **model** how to draw a response to the words: *Little by little, change happens.* Example:

6. **Ask** participants to draw, on page 10, what "Little by little, change happens" means to them in terms of time management.

7. **Ask** participants to briefly share their responses.

Be Flexible

There is no right way to draw a response. Participants come up with wonderfully creative ways to illustrate their thinking.

Look out for perfectionist artists. Tell them that this is not the time for drawing perfect little pictures. A basic outline or sketch is what you want.

If students are really stuck when faced with drawing, let it go and let them write words. We want to encourage people to use their mind's strength during this process.

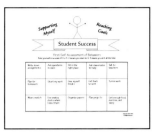

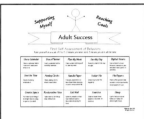

Pages 11–12:
First Self-Assessments

The self-assessment process is the first step toward building an awareness of the connection between choices and time management. The self-assessment score isn't important. What is, is beginning to reflect and think about various aspects of time management needed to successfully get things done.

There are two self-assessment forms. One is for students, on page 11. The other is for adults, on page 12. When working with families, guide students through their page and let the parents work independently.

MATERIALS NEEDED:

Self-Assessment Comparison form for each participant (In the appendix)

WHAT I DO:

1. **Direct** participants to page 11 for students; and page 12 for adults.

2. **Explain** that in terms of time management and organization, there are fifteen separate behaviors that support being a successful student and a successful adult. Each behavior has its own box.

ACTIVITY:

Ask participants to rate themselves in each behavior box on a scale of 0 to 5. Zero means they never do it. Five means they do it all the time. Explain that in coming sessions, most box topics will be discussed in detail.

NOTE: You will want to fill in a Self-Assessment Comparison form for each participant (In the appendix). You can either do this as the clients fill in their own score or after the session is over if the workbooks are left in your office between sessions.

Tip

This course does not focus on these three important subjects: sleep, food, and exercise. Take some time here to mention that good time management is dependent upon the brain, which *needs* around nine hours of sleep per night for an adolescent (eight for an adult). It also requires energy from good food at appropriate intervals and responds positively to physical exercise. For more information refer clients to the book *Brain Rules* by John Medina.

Page 13:
Executive Skills

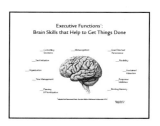

Page 13 in the *Course Notes* provides a list of eleven executive functioning skills (around an illustration of the brain) adapted from *Executive Skills in Children and Adolescents* by Peg Dawson and Richard Guare. It is important to discuss each of these skills with your clients, using the talking points given under each executive skill in this manual. You will be asking them to reflect upon each skill and assess whether it is a personal strength or weakness. This knowledge makes it possible for the clients to begin to see their time-management issues as having a biological basis.

Listed here are general talking points about executive functioning. This is followed by more specific information about each of the eleven executive functioning skills.

As you look at page 13 you will begin your explanations with the word *metacognition* and then work around the brain in a clockwise direction, ending with the words *controlling emotions*.

WHAT I DO:

1. **Direct** participants to page 13.

2. **Provide** the following information to the participants:

    - Executive functioning skills are the result of the interactions of at least eleven different skills.

    - Executive functioning processes affect one's ability to get things done.

    - A weakness in any area will cause problems.

    - The more areas of weakness, the greater the challenges for time management.

    - Almost everyone has a weakness in one or more executive skills. There is no such thing as a perfect brain.

3. **Explain** that participants will be considering each executive skill and rating it as a personal strength or a weakness.

Definition

At present, there is no official standardized definition of what makes up specific executive functioning skills. It depends upon the researcher. I've chosen to use the breakdown created by Dawson and Guare in *Executive Skills in Children and Adolescents*, 2010.

Tip

As I go through this page, I share with my clients my personal areas of weak executive functioning, assuring them that everyone, every brain, has strengths and weaknesses. In *Click: The Magic of Instant Connections*, by the Brafam brothers, it is explained that when we are willing to share our personal vulnerability, we increase the odds of "clicking" with another person. I believe that by sharing stories about my own imperfect brain, I am able to improve my connections with my clients, especially defensive adolescents.

4. **Direct** participants to the word *metacognition* above the illustration of the brain. Use the talking points for metacognition listed here and allow participants to score themselves. Continue clockwise around the brain, describing each executive skill.

Metacognition

Explain the following points about metacognition:

- Metacognition is the first of the three executive skills that dominate the interactions of the other skills.

- *Metacognition* is basically defined as "thinking about your thinking."

- It is that voice in your head that reflects on your actions, providing options or choices as you think about your own behavior.

- It is akin to an awareness of self, or pausing to look at what you are doing.

- In many ways, the time-challenged are unconscious of the connection between their behavior and time management.

- Generating metacognition connected to time is the goal of *The Sklar Process*. **It is the development of metacognition that creates long-lasting behavior change connected to time management.**

Ask: Are you able to stop doing what you want to be doing to do something you don't want to do?

Direct participants to give themselves a + or a – on the line in front of the word *metacognition* on page 13.

Goal-Directed Persistence

Explain the following points about goal-directed persistence:

- If you have goal-directed persistence, you can stick with a task through to completion.

- You finish your math homework instead of wandering off and forgetting to come back to finish it.

- You finish projects instead of having partially completed projects lying around.

Ask: Do you finish projects instead of having partially completed projects lying around?

Direct participants to give themselves a + or a – on the line in front of the words *goal-directed persistence*.

Flexibility

Explain the following about flexibility:

- This is not about the kind of flexibility developed in yoga or gymnastics. This refers to flexible thinking.

- You try a different approach when you are stuck.

Ask: Do you have trouble transitioning, changing from one activity or task to another?

Direct participants to give themselves a + or a – on the line in front of the word *flexibility*.

Sustained Attention

Explain the following points about sustained attention:

- The ability to stay focused on a task defines sustained attention.

- The ability to sustain focus can be task specific, especially for the ADHD mind.

Ask: Are you able to stay focused on tasks you don't like as well as tasks you do like?

Direct participants to give themselves a + or a – on the line in front of the words *sustained attention*.

Response Inhibition

Explain the following points about response inhibition:

- Response inhibition is another way of saying controlling impulsive behavior.

- This is connected to being easily distracted by your environment and not having the metacognitive ability to tell yourself: "No, not now," or, "This is not a good thing to do."

Ask: Are you able to stop yourself from blurting out in class?

Direct participants to give themselves a + or a – on the line in front of the words *response inhibition.*

Working Memory

Explain the following points about working memory:

- Working memory is another critical executive skill that directly impacts the effectiveness and efficiency of the other skills.

- Working memory is that part of our thinking process where we keep track of information to use, like a notepad. An example is being able to multiply 56 and 37 in your head. Another example is being able to remember directions to somewhere you've never been. If you have trouble doing these things without writing it down, you have challenges with working memory.

- Most people can keep track of about seven "chunks" of information at a time.

- Described it as being like the hub in a road system. All of the other executive skills (roads) converge and have to pass through working memory.

- If you have a diminished working memory capacity, you are going to have more challenges with time management.

- As we age, our working memory decreases, which explains the phenomenon of people who could once keep everything they needed to do in their heads suddenly finding that they need to write things down and check calendars.

Ask: Are you able to remember all the directions a teacher tells without forgetting a step and without writing them down?

Direct participants to give themselves a + or a – on the line in front of the words *working memory.*

Planning and Prioritization

Explain the following points about planning and prioritization:

- •Planning refers to breaking a complicated task into steps or smaller pieces to work on. Examples would be planning out the steps of writing a term paper or painting a room.

- •Prioritization refers to deciding which step or activity is the most important to do next.

Ask: Are you able to break a big project into steps and get it done on time?

Direct participants to give themselves a + or a – on the line in front of the words *planning and prioritization*.

Time Management

Explain the following points about time management:

- •Time management requires individuals to have an internal awareness of the passing of time.

- •Without this awareness, we are prone to make poor choices in how we use our time.

Ask: Are you able to use your time well by doing your work before you play?

Direct participants to give themselves a + or a – on the line in front of the words *time management*.

Organization

Explain the following points about organization:

- •Organization can refer to two things: organizing thoughts in our mind and organizing things like papers and our belongings in our room or home.

- •Are papers constantly misplaced or lost?

- •Are there disorganized piles everywhere?

- •Are things like keys and cell phones constantly misplaced?

- Do you have trouble organizing your writing projects into paragraphs with topic sentences supported by details?

Ask: Are you able to keep track of all the little things in your life?

Direct participants to give themselves a + or a − on the line in front of the word *organization*.

Task Initiation

Explain the following points about task initiation:

- The opposite of task initiation is procrastination, putting things off.

- The time-challenged are labeled procrastinators from an early age.

Ask: Are you able to get started on things you don't want to do without being asked?

Direct participants to give themselves a + or − on the line in front of the words *task initiation*.

Controlling Emotions

Explain the following points about controlling emotions:

- The ability to control emotions is the third executive skill that can greatly affect the other skills required to get things done.

- It is important to properly diagnose why someone is not getting work done.

- In fact, depression, fear, anxiety, and anger will dominate and override the ability of the other executive functioning skills to manage behavior.

- Don't overlook anxiety, depression, and anger as the underlying source of the problem.

Ask: Are you able to keep working when you don't feel like it?

Direct participants to give themselves a + or a − on the line in front of the words *controlling emotions*.

Page 14:
What I Need to Understand About the Brain and Learners

Pages 14 and 15 are the foundation for *The Sklar Process*. Critical background knowledge is introduced that will be referred to as the course progresses. Each topic adds to the participants' understanding of their past behavior connected to not getting things done. It is very powerful for the time-challenged to finally have explanations for their behavior. It gives them a different perspective on themselves and provides the opening for hope that they can change their future behavior by participating in the course.

There is a lot of content on these pages, which requires a lot of words to explain. However, remember a picture is worth a thousand words. Each topic has a drawn visual example that will help you both understand the directions and help your clients understand your explanations. As you read the directions, look at the drawings. Practice making your own drawing of the idea.

In order not to lose your participants in this first session, **you must draw to back up your words.** Your drawings allow the participants to pause and reflect upon important ideas and concepts and meet the needs of the visual learner.

With each term, ask the participants to copy your drawings in the appropriate spaces on pages 14 and 15.

Metacognition

Metacognition is a challenging idea to get across to people. It is difficult to think about your thinking. How do you do that? Folks with ADHD and executive functioning deficits often lack the ability to observe their own behavior and thought processes. It is very foreign to them.

A trait of this population is to move through life reacting to stimuli in the environment. They often don't pause to consider a response. They don't think before they act. As a result, pausing is also a foreign concept. In order to begin thinking about your thinking and develop metacognition, you need to be able to pause.

How do you teach pausing? The answer came in a yoga class.

Pausing in Yoga and Life

My yoga instructor, Todd Williamson, often leads his class through the following guided-breathing exercise. The purpose is to develop an awareness of our breath going in and out—focusing on how there is a "pause point" just as the breathing process goes from inhaling to exhaling and vice versa. Todd teaches that it is during this brief pause point, that we have the power of choice over our reactions to the events in our daily life.

I'd been listening to Todd's guided meditation for years when I had the *ah-ha!* moment. I'd teach about pausing and metacognition using a breathing exercise. It works.

WHAT I DO:

1. **Direct** participants to page 14 and the word *metacognition*.

2. **Explain** that the next two pages are critical background knowledge needed to change time-management behavior.

3. **Explain** the following points:

    • Developing metacognition connected to time management is a fundamental goal of this program.

    • A simple definition for metacognition is "thinking about your thinking."

    • Draw on the dry erase board an image of a person thinking about their thinking. Example:

Tip

One of my adolescent clients told me that thinking about your thinking is hard—it's like looking in a mirror while you are holding a mirror. Where do you begin and end?

4. **Explain** that it is rather strange to try to think about your thinking.

   • Usually the time-challenged just move through their day, unconscious of the impact of their time-management decisions.

   • The first step to developing metacognition is to pause and pay attention to the decision points that you usually zip right past.

Teaching How to Pause

WHAT I DO

1. **Announce** that you are going to teach about pausing by using a yoga breathing exercise. Ask them to follow these directions:

   Close your eyes.
   Breathe out all the air from your lungs and hold it out for a couple of seconds.
   Now, let the breath of air rush in and fill your lungs.
   Stop. Add a little more breath. Hold it.
   Now push out all the air and hold it out.
   Let go and let the air rush in.
   Breathe out. Hold.
   Breathe in. Hold.
   Now I want you to breathe normally, but pay attention to the point where the breath changes from going in to going out.
   It's a little like being in a roller coaster as you reach the top and suddenly are going down.

   Do this quiet breathing a couple of times.
   Open your eyes.

2. **Explain** that the point where the breath changes directions is a little tiny pause point.

3. **Encourage** your participants to begin noticing the pause points in their thinking, just as they can notice the pause points in their breathing.

4. **Explain** that metacognition is really pausing to think about your thinking. Like learning anything new, it takes practice to start paying attention to your thinking.

5. **Add** the word *pause* to your drawing of thinking about your thinking. Example:

Tip

After writing the word "pause," direct participants to write the word "choice" next to "pause" and connect the two words with an arrow. This pause point is our choice point where behavior changes.

ACTIVITY:

1. **Direct** participants to page 14.

2. Under the word *metacognition,* **ask** them to draw what they now know about metacognition.

Brain Development

A discussion about brain development is critical for college-aged adults and adolescents with their parents. Through brain-imaging technologies, we can now prove what car insurance companies have known for years: the average person doesn't have a fully developed, neurologically wired prefrontal cortex until the average age of twenty-five. Most car rental agencies won't rent a car to someone under that age because drivers under twenty-five have a substantially higher rate of car accidents.

What brain activity is predominately in the prefrontal cortex? It's the location of the wiring for our executive functioning skills, the part of the brain that makes behavior choices, cares about time, does long-term planning, etc.

Unfortunately, as a society, we expect young people between the ages of twelve and twenty-five to behave as if they have an adult brain. Since they don't have an adult brain, they can't consistently make time-management choices that adults expect them to make. We are setting these young people up to fail by having unrealistic expectations, which are at the root of many conflicts between teens and parents, as well as school failure.

By providing this knowledge to adolescents and parents, you accomplish at least two things. First, you take the blame away from the time-challenged, since their difficulties stem in part from their brain and not their free will in choosing to not get things done. This is another release of guilt and shame.

The second thing you do is help the parents get a realistic and honest view of the next few years of their life. Their child is going to need their support to develop time-management skills. Most adolescents can't do it alone, and most schools are not providing the necessary support. Parents need to provide support, either through their own efforts or by paying for those of a life coach or mentor.

Tip
Executive Skills in Children and Adolescents, by Dawson and Guare, has a chapter on the value of coaching students with executive skills deficits.

WHAT I DO:

1. On the dry erase board **draw** a picture of a side view of the brain. Example:

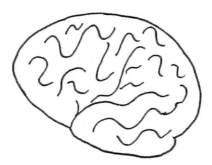

2. **Explain** the following points:

   • The brain is an incredibly complex network of "wiring," or neuron connections that control our behavior.

   • The main wiring for executive functioning skills is primarily located in the front of the brain—the prefrontal cortex.

About Drawing
My drawings of the brain have been described as looking like a raisin or a walnut.

3. **Draw** a curve separating the prefrontal cortex from the rest of your brain drawing. Example:

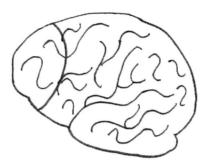

4. **Explain** that because of our ability to now take pictures of the brain in action, we know that the wiring in the prefrontal cortex is the last part of the brain to fully develop.

5. **Erase** the area of the prefrontal cortex from the board so it is blank and empty of lines. Example:

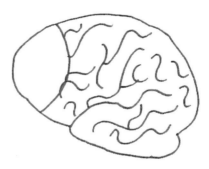

6. **Ask** each participant to guess how old you have to be before you have a fully developed grown-up brain.

7. **Give** the correct answer: the average age is twenty-five. Write *Grown-up brain age* next to your drawing of the brain. Example:

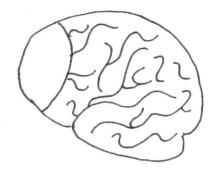

Grown-up Brain → 25 years old

Dramatization for Family Groups

To bring this abstract bit of knowledge back to the lives of family members, I pause and do a little dramatization as I tell a story. It's about what happens to parents on back-to-school night at the beginning of middle school.

Parents are told by a school authority figure that it is time for their child to grow up and become independent of their parents' help in managing homework. This little skit points out how the parent and child were both set up for conflict and failure by that well-meaning school authority who was acting on folklore versus science.

This interaction about brain development is crucial to help teens get past resistance to the program. It is another step in relieving the years of guilt experienced by the time-challenged. It is the beginning of accepting that their executive functioning issues are brain-based. Parents discover how they have unwittingly been part of the problem.

It also changes how the parent and child view their past conflicts over time management and homework, and it opens up the opportunity to change that pattern in the future.

WHAT I DO:

1. **Walk over to the parents,** addressing the following dialogue to them.

   When your child started middle school, you likely attended

a parent night at which an authority figure stood before the parents and told you something like the following:

It is time for your children to grow up and accept responsibility for getting their homework done and turned in on time. You need to back out. They will learn from their mistakes.

Did this happen to you? (They'll nod yes.)

Now that you know the brain doesn't fully develop until age twenty-five, should you have pulled back on your support? (They'll shake their head no.)

2. **Turn to the students** and address them.

Do you have a brain that is fully ready to manage your time and your stuff like an adult does? (They will shake their head no.)

That's right. Your brain wasn't—isn't—ready to think about time management like an adult.

This is good news for you. You are not a bad, lazy person. You cannot do what your brain cannot do.

3. **Turn back to the parents.**

This is bad news for you.

You are going to have to stay involved with your children's time management as they develop the neuron connections in their prefrontal cortex to independently manage time.

They need your support. You don't do their work for them, but you have to support them.

We'll be talking more about how to do that in later sessions.

4. **Tell** participants that you invite them to each reconsider how they interrelate about using time.

5. **Turn to the children.**

You might do well to accept the fact that it is OK to get reminders and help from your parent, because that is how you are

Think About It

We don't expect the physically handicapped, who need a wheelchair, to just try harder to get up and walk. Nor should we blame the time-challenged for their executive functioning deficits that are brain based.

51

going to grow the brain wiring to become fully independent by age twenty-five.

6. **Turn to the parents.**

You are going to have to put some thought into how to support your child's executive functioning skill development so that they can transition first into college or living on their own and eventually become a fully independent adult.

It is going to take years. (Parents don't like hearing this. But it is the honest truth.)

ACTIVITY:

Ask participants to please draw what they have learned about brain development on page 14.

Sound Brain or Picture Brain *

Today it is very common for people to identify themselves as visual, auditory, or kinesthetic (tactile) learners. I decided to label the different kinds of learners as either having a CD brain (an auditory learner) or a DVD brain (visual with a kinesthetic component). I introduce this topic to encourage the visual learners to use their visual strength to experiment with drawing their notes. It also opens discussion about how they should ask for help in learning situations—asking teachers to show what they have just talked about.

WHAT I DO:

1. **Explain** the following:

   • People have different learning styles and strengths.

   • The way people think is really complex.

   • The following simplified model shows how people think differently.

2. On the dry erase board **draw** a new side view of the brain. Example:

*Analogy Alert

For years, and in this instructor's manual, I have used a visual analogy of comparing a CD to a DVD to explain the differences between an auditory thinking brain and a visual thinking brain. With technology becoming outdated overnight, the day is coming when using a CD and DVD will no longer make sense to a younger generation.

My best advice is to stay current with technology and judge the age and knowledge of your participants. At the publication of this edition, (2013), a good substitute would be to compare an iPod (a sound-only device) with an iTouch or iPad (visual and kinesthetic devices). This comparison would be easy to draw in place of the circular CD and DVD images.

Be flexible and be sure your audience understands that you are talking about the difference between the visual and auditory strengths of a brain.

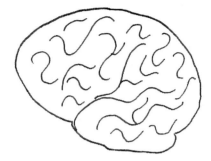

3. **Draw** two concentric circles to represent a CD over part of the brain. Label it CD. Example:

Tip

Use differently colored markers to differentiate between the CD brain and the DVD brain. This will give a better picture for the visual thinker to remember.

4. **Explain** the following:

   • Some people have what I call a CD brain.

   • CD brains learn easily by listening.

   • CD brains store their thoughts in sounds. It's like pushing a button to hear a recording of a teacher's lecture.

   For instance, if you were starting your science homework, you would pause and think, "What did Ms. Jones say about this? Oh, yes, track seven."

5. **Explain** that this drawing will show them how a CD brain gets information into memory.

   • To the right, above the brain, **draw a stick figure** with a speech bubble. Inside the speech bubble write: *Yak, yak, yak…*I tell participants that teachers are yak-yakers. I always get nods of agreement.)

53

• Next, **draw an ear** to the right of the brain.

• Then, **draw a connecting arrow** from the speech bubble, through the ear, to the drawing of the CD. Example:

6. **Explain** that other people, like the author of this book, have what is called a DVD brain.

7. **Draw** another circle on the brain, this time to represent a DVD. Label it DVD.

8. **Draw** a large eye and a hand. Connect them with arrows to the DVD symbol on the brain. Example:

9. **Explain** the following:

• People with DVD brains store their thoughts in pictures.

• DVD people learn best using their eyes and their body.

In a class I recently learned that current research tells us that ninety percent of us learn best with information presented visually. This makes sense since more of our brain is dedicated to our visual sensory system compared to our auditory system.

I now share this information with my participants. After discussing their personal strengths, I write 90% on the dry erase board next to the eye. Then I ask the question: *looking at the dry erase board, what is wrong with this picture?*

The correct response is that teachers who "yak-yak" are only meeting the needs of ten percent of the students in their classrooms. A person in business would be a failure if they only met the needs of ten percent of the customers who walk in the door. There needs to be a change.

• They need visual examples to store in their memory.

• This means that yak-yaking teachers are not a good match for visual learners unless they back up their words with visuals.

• It helps if DVD people do something with their body while they are focusing on learning, like drawing their notes instead of sitting passively while listening.

10. **Ask** each participant: which brain do you think you have? (If they can't answer, let them know that is OK. Invite them to start thinking about what makes learning easiest for them: hearing instructions or being shown how to do something.)

11. **Explain** that this is a way to think about what your learning strengths might be. You want to use tools and strategies that match your strengths.

ACTIVITY:

Ask participants to please draw what they've learned about sound and picture brains on page 14.

What Is Learning?

Most people are unaware of what is going on in the brain when we learn something new. This very simple model helps explain what is happening in the brain as we connect new learning to past learning. It also helps to explain why we have trouble learning something in a brand-new subject. We lack prior experience to connect it to the brain's memory.

WHAT I DO:

1. **Explain** that this is a simplified way of thinking about what goes on in the brain when we learn something new.

2. **Draw** a side view of the brain.

3. **Draw,** in a different color, a small triangle over some area of the brain. Example:

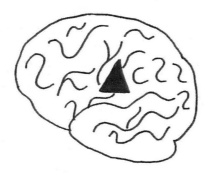

4. **Say:** Somewhere back when you were a little kid, you learned to identify a triangle as a shape with three sides.

5. **Draw** a picture of a pyramid shape below the brain. Example:

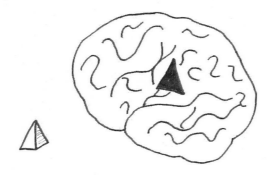

6. **Say:** Years later you were shown a pyramid. When you saw the new shape, your brain went—"Oh, that is sort of like a triangle. Let's hook this new idea about a pyramid to the old idea of a triangle."

7. **Draw** an arrow that connects the pyramid to the triangle in the brain. Example:

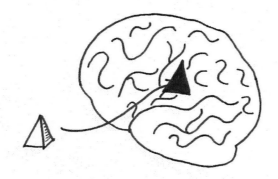

Resource

Check out *Brain Rules* by John Medina for highly readable information about neurons and the brain. I've bought lots of books about the brain. This is the only one I've read cover to cover, twice, taking notes the second time.

Tip

If you are working with high school and college students who struggle in specific subjects, recommend that they purchase a DVD on the subject at www.teach12.com. Use the DVD as an introduction to brand-new subjects, or as a boost for challenging subjects, in order to have some kind background *before* they take the class for credit.

8. **Say:** As you learn something, your brain builds new connections between neurons. When you practice something or review it, the neuron connections in the brain get stronger.

9. **Explain** that this is important to know because it explains why some things are so hard to learn. For example many students find their first chemistry class challenging because they've never really studied anything quite like it. They don't have a lot of previous experiences with chemistry stored away in the brain.

10. On the board below the brain, **write:** *Learning is connecting new information to old information in the brain.*

ACTIVITY:

Direct participants to draw what they have learned about learning on page 14.

Page 15:
More to Understand

The Learning and Behavior Connection

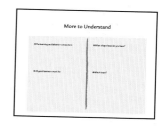

Traditionally when we are faced with a student's unsuccessful or negative behavior connected to school, we explain the source of the behavior using one or two models.

There is the medical model that explains that there is something wrong with the physiology of the brain. Often a medication is prescribed to help the situation. The other model comes out of psychology, suggesting that the problem is rooted in the family of origin.

These models explain some of what we see with struggling learners, but there is a third model that needs to be considered. It is a model that connects behavior to mastery and competency in learning environments.

I got the idea for this model from a workshop presented by psychologist Matthew O'Byrne titled, "Mastery and Competence—The Foundations of Self." This model is often the most powerful and moving information for my clients. It is consistently the key take-home idea for parents.

WHAT I DO:

1. **Direct** participants to page 15.

2. **Explain:**

    • There are two traditional ways to explain our behavior—the medical model and the psychological model based on family of origin.

    • In the medical model, if something is wrong, you are often encouraged to take a pill to help solve the problem. It can help.

    • In the psychology model you are told that if you just had a better parent, you'd be fine. (As a mother, I joke that I don't buy this model.)

Resource

As a member of the Association of Educational Therapists (AET), I have attended valuable workshops and conferences, including "Developmental and Emotional Factors in Learning: Mastery and Competence—the Foundation of Self" where Matthew O'Byrne was one of five presenters. He is a clinical psychologist in a group practice in San Rafael, California. I'm forever grateful for the idea of the connection between our emotional response to learning and our behavior.

- Both of these models may explain some of our behaviors. However, there is a third very compelling and powerful model to explain some behavior.

3. **Write** on the top of the dry erase board: *Learning and Behavior*.

4. In the top left corner **draw** a confused character. Example:

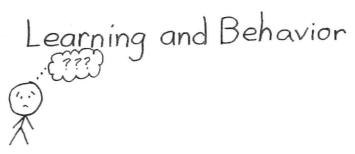

- **Explain** that whenever we learn something new, brand new, our first emotional response is to feel confused. Being confused happens to everyone whenever they are challenged to learn something new.

- Under the words *Learning and Behavior*, **add a bullet point** followed by the word c*onfused*. Example:

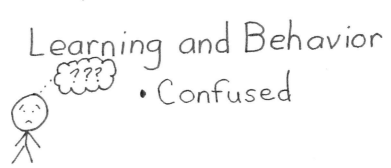

5. **Explain** that if the confusion isn't cleared up, our next emotional response is to feel helpless. We think, "I can't do this."

- Under the word *confused* **add a bullet point** and write the word *helpless*.

- Draw an arrow connecting confused to helpless. Example:

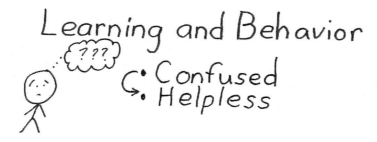

6. **Explain** that if the confusion still isn't cleared up, then our next emotional response is to feel hopeless. We think, "I will never be able to do this."

   •Under the word *helpless* **add a bullet point** and write the word *hopeless*.

   •**Draw** an arrow to connect helpless to hopeless. Example:

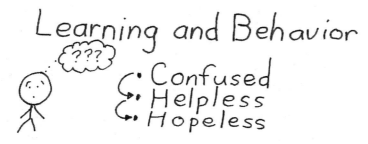

7. **Ask:** Are the emotions of confusion, helplessness, and hopelessness comfortable feelings? (Participants will shake their heads no.)

8. **Respond:** Correct. We don't like these feelings. We want to avoid them. They are painful.

9. **Explain:**

   •The brain is designed to protect us.

   •Strong emotions activate our primal drive of fight or flight.

   •To get away from pain, we are motivated by the brain to do something.

10. **Explain:** Psychologists would say that the pain motivates a behavior.

- Under the word *hopeless* **add a bullet point** and write the word *behavior*.

- **Draw** an arrow connecting the word *hopeless* with the word *behavior*. Example:

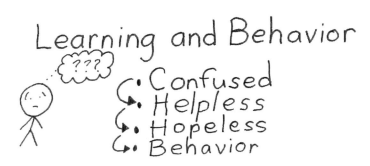

11. **Say:** Our brain has several behavioral choices to get away from the pain.

- **Draw** an arrow pointing down and to the left of the word *behavior*.

- **Write** the word *escape* below the arrow. Example:

A Story of Escape

I had a twelve-year-old reading student who had severe dyslexia. After just a few weeks in middle school, he ran away. He couldn't take the humiliation, frustration, and failure he was experiencing. He was gone for over three days before the police found him breaking into his grandmother's home with a new buddy from his special education class.

12. **Explain:** Escaping the pain is a common choice. Escape can look like lots of things.

- It can be throwing a wad of paper at a classmate to distract the teacher.

- It can be text messaging or reading a book instead of paying attention in class.

- It can be spending time on Facebook instead of doing homework.

- It can be lying about having done your work.

- In more severe cases it is literally running away from school and home.

13. **Draw** another arrow pointing down from the word *behavior*. Write the word *anger*. Example:

14. **Explain:** Anger is a quick defensive response to pain.

- It is the fight response versus the flight response of escape.

- This is the teenager exploding when asked about her homework.

- This is the basis of the rants about stupid teachers and parents that won't "get off my back so I can just do my work."

- The statement: "Just leave me alone!" may actually be covering up some point of confusion.

15. **Draw** an arrow pointing down from the word *behavior*. **Write** the words *depression and anxiety*. Example:

Think About It

I've often wondered if trying to escape the pain of academic failure is the starting point for drug and alcohol abuse for some young people. It is probably the source of a lot "sick" students who don't make it to school.

Tip

I advise parents that the next time their adolescent gives them inappropriate behavior connected to school, they should pause, take a deep breath, and ask themselves, "I wonder where the confusion is. What doesn't my child see or understand?"

When the child calms down, the parents can then ask, "You seem stuck or confused about this assignment. How I can help you clear up the confusion?"

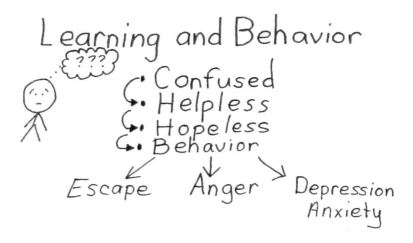

16. **Explain** the following:

- Depression and anxiety are very serious responses to the pain connected to challenges with learning.

- Hopelessness can manifest itself in depression.

- Fear of repeating failure brings on anxiety.

- Individuals may want to change their behavior but are unable to because depression or anxiety overpowers their ability to act. These individuals may need professional psychological interventions.

17. **Draw** a seated person below the words *escape, anger, depression* and *anxiety*. Cover the figure's eyes, and then draw a barred cage over the figure. Example:

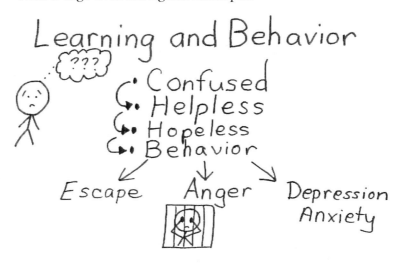

18. **Explain** the following:

- This represents a wounded learner.

- After years of feeling confused, helpless, and hopeless, a brain and its body can succumb and become a wounded learner.

- Wounded learners are dominated by pain connected to years of learning struggles.

- A wounded learner is at serious risk for school and work failure.

- Their self-esteem suffers.

- They may never reach their full potential.

- They don't believe that they can be successful learners or successful people.

19. **Proclaim:** But there is hope!

- **Draw** a line representing a trap door coming off one corner of the cage.

- **Explain:** There is a trap door that can help the wounded learner escape. Example:

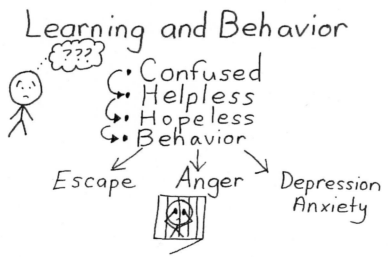

20. **Explain:** The key for having hope is to go back to the second emotion we described earlier: helpless.

Resource

Carol Dweck, professor of psychology at Stanford and author of *Mindset: The New Psychology of Success,* presents empirical evidence supporting the fact that our personal beliefs about our abilities determine what we accomplish in life. *Mindset* is an interesting book to read.

- **Draw** an arrow from the bottom of the cage up to the word *helpless*. Example:

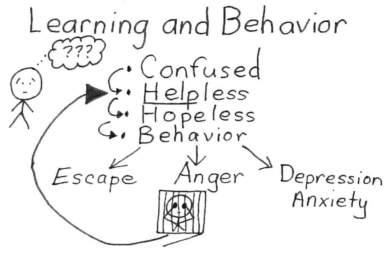

- **Ask:** What is the root word for *helpless*?

- **The answer:** Help. Underline the root word *help*.

21. **Explain** that in most learning situations, we need to get help at some point or another. We rely on the knowledge and experience of others to help us solve the problems of connecting new information to old information in our brain.

- **Draw** two stick figures in the top right corner of the board. Have them holding hands. Getting help and clearing up the confusion is where learning happens.

- **Draw** an arrow from the underlined word *help* to the two characters. Example:

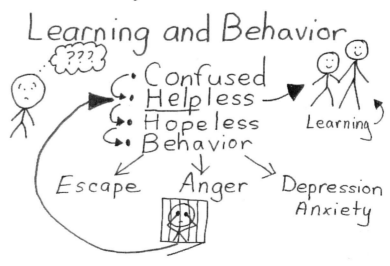

22. **Ask:** Have any of you ever experienced this connection between your behavior and a challenging learning situation? (Heads will nod yes.)

ACTIVITY:

Direct participants to draw on page 15 about the connection between learning and behavior, including the points on the dry erase board.

All Good Learners Must Be:

To be successful, students need to nurture the two qualities of honesty and courage. They have to be honest with others and themselves when they are confused and don't understand something being taught. They have to have courage because many students find raising their hand in class and admitting that they don't understand something to be threatening. They are insecure and don't want classmates to know that they are not "capable" or "smart." Lacking this honesty or courage sets up school failure.

WHAT I DO:

1. **Say:** Successful learners have to have two qualities.

    • **Write** the word *honesty* on the board.

    • **Explain** this is the first quality necessary to be successful.

    • **Ask:** What do students need to be honest about?

    • **Answer:** You need to be honest about when you need to get help. You have to admit you are confused.

2. **Write** the word *courage* on the board.

    • Explain this is the second quality necessary to be a successful learner (or a successful adult).

    • **Ask:** Why do good students have to be courageous?

    • **Answer:** It takes courage to ask for help. You run the risk of letting others think that you aren't smart and capable.

3. **Explain:** Many teenagers and young adults would rather fail in school than ask for help.

Resource

The idea of connecting the traits of honesty and courage to being a successful learner came from Tim McGee's DVD *How to Become a SuperStar Student*.

Tip

When working with families, I take the opportunity to dramatize the following situation for adolescents: I flatten myself against the wall and explain this is how adolescents in middle school and early high school feel. They want to blend into the wall and not stand out. As adults and parents, it is easy for us to say, "Just ask your teacher." For adolescents, this is a situation that may be fraught with powerful conflicting emotions. They don't want anyone to think they are not capable or not smart.

Think About It

I had a twenty-year-old student beginning his third attempt at college. I asked him if he'd ever raised his hand in class or gone to the professor when he was confused. His answer: no.

A Story of Courage

I had a ninth-grader who was failing a social studies class. She complained that she just didn't understand the teacher—he was a yak-yakker, and she was a visual learner. Since she was a young woman with a strong sense of herself, I suggested that when she was confused in his lecture, she should raise her hand and tell him so. Then she should let him know it would be helpful to her if he could draw on the board to help her understand the concept. She and I spent thirty minutes of role-playing (me being the teacher) so she could practice how to ask that teacher for clarification and help.

When she came back the next week, I inquired about how it had worked when she'd asked for help. Her answer: "It was *amazing*!"

I wasn't expecting such enthusiasm, so I said, "He drew on the board so you could understand?"

"Oh, yeah. That wasn't what was so amazing. What was amazing was when class was over and I was leaving, all of these kids gathered around me and treated me like I was smart."

My student had had the courage to ask for help—help a lot of the other students in the room needed too. Of course they saw her as brave and deserving of respect.

ACTIVITY:

Direct participants to draw or write on page 15 about the two qualities a good learner must have.

What Shape Head Do You Have?

Students with executive functioning challenges and learning differences struggle with low self-esteem as learners. It is helpful to reframe the problem for them. I came up with the following visual story to explain that while their brain is not a match for school, it may be the perfect brain to be successful outside of school. The challenge is to not become wounded learners and thus give up believing in their own potential. It is a very popular model and helps to encourage self-acceptance and hope.

WHAT I DO:

1. **Say:** This is a model to give you a way to think about the school environment and yourself as a learner.

- **Draw** a rectangle shape to represent a school.

- **Write** the word *school* across the top.

- **Draw** a doorway that is the shape of an old-fashioned key-hole. Example:

2. **Explain** that you think of the typical school as a building that has a keyhole-shaped doorway.

3. **Draw** a lollipop head stick figure below the door. Example:

4. **Explain** the following:

   - If you are person with a lollipop head, you are going to fit perfectly in school.

   - The lollipop head isn't better than anyone else. It just happens to be the right match for the typical school environment and expectations.

5. **Draw** a stick figure with an oval-shaped head. Example:

6. **Tell** the following story to describe an oval head. (If you identify yourself as not being a lollipop head, then by all means, insert your own story here.)

The author of this book describes herself as having an oval-shaped head. She didn't have any sharp corners that caused problems in school. She made sure that she kept everybody's attention on her strengths. She hid her weaknesses, which included time management, organization, a limited working memory, all things connected to numbers, and serious challenges organizing her writing assignments. (And she went on to become an author!)

7. **Draw** a variety of differently shaped heads on stick figures to the left of the school.

- Draw a triangle-shaped head.

- Draw a polygon-shaped head.

- Draw a dodecahedron head (or something like it). Explain that this is the kind of head somebody extraordinary like Bill Gates or Steve Jobs might have. Example:

8. **Ask** participants to describe the shape of their head. Answers are going to vary. Acknowledge there is no right answer. It's just a barometer showing everyone how much of a match they felt they are/were for school.

9. **Ask:** What shaped heads do you suppose most teachers have?

   •**Draw** a lollipop stick figure to the right above the school and label it *teacher*. Example:

   •**Explain** that most teachers are lollipop heads. They loved school. They were a match. So of course they would want to spend their adult lives there.

   •This is not a put-down of teachers. Good teachers work really hard. It's just that some of them have trouble relating to the needs of students with different-shaped heads.

A Head Story

When asked to describe the shape of her head, one of my students came up to the dry erase board to draw her answer. She drew an oval head with a small pointed horn. I loved it!

10. **Draw** a triangle head stick figure to the right of the school, below the teacher figure. Example below:

  - **Draw** an arrow connecting the triangle head on the left side of the school, going across the school building and pointing to the newest triangle head.
  - **Explain** that it is very important, and challenging, for people who don't have lollipop heads to get through school with their hearts and confidence intact, feeling like capable learners.

  - **Draw** a heart over the body of the triangle head on the right. Example:

11. **Explain** that here is an important truth about the world outside of schools.

  - **Draw** a box with dollar signs over it.

  - **Draw** different head shapes in the box. Example:

71

- **Explain** that in the world where we make money, businesses don't want rooms full of just lollipop heads.

12. **Explain** that the world has really changed because of technology. A lot of the things that lollipop heads do well—that schools stress, like learning facts—computers do faster and better, and people in India do more cheaply. Because of these changes, our businesses and our country need the skills and strengths and creativity of differently shaped heads.

13. **Explain** that it is wonderful that we need all these different kinds of creative minds. However, there is a big problem:

   - Many of these creative and different kinds of minds have executive functioning challenges. They may have trouble getting things done on time.

   - Success in business and life comes down to getting things done well and on time. Creative, bright people are in trouble if they don't develop good time-management skills.

   - By being in this course, participants are setting themselves up for future success! They'll have the tools for good time management that they will need.

14. **Recap** these points:

   - Schools are primarily designed for one kind of mind.

   - Struggles in school may come from the mismatch between a particular brain and the school environment.

   - Just because your mind isn't a match for a school doesn't mean you aren't a capable learner.

   - If you develop good time-management skills, you are setting yourself up for a successful life.

ACTIVITY:

Ask participants to draw on page 15 about differently shaped heads.

Which Train?

So far, the emphasis of this course has been to remove the shame

Resource

Daniel Pink, in his book, *A Whole New Mind: Why Right-Brainers Will Rule the Future*, presents compelling arguments that in order to maintain our standard of living—to be employable—we in the United States need to develop skills that are not necessarily those encouraged by our traditional school systems.

Resources

What motivates people is an interesting topic. Two thoughtful books to read are:

Drive: The Surprising Truth About What Motivates Us by Daniel Pink.

Mindset: The New Psychology of Success by Carol Dweck. This books stresses the connection between success and effort.

and guilt for the time-challenged. However, there is definitely a need to address the whole issue of will, of choice. There comes a point in this process that the participants have to choose to do the work necessary to support their time-challenged brain.

The idea for "Which Train?" comes from master teacher and consultant Rhonda Birnie. Every September she'd tell her elementary students that they have a choice in school (and in life) to get on one of two trains: the E-Train or the L-Train.

The following analogy may strike some people as politically incorrect and insensitive because it uses the word *lazy*. However, the point of this example is to emphasize that we all have to make a choice to be successful. We have to work to be successful. In fact, I tell my students and clients with learning disabilities that in order for them to be successful, they are going to have to work harder than most people around them. They can't afford to choose to slack off. It is the honest truth.

The clients who choose the trains as their key idea for the session are often the ones who need to be honest and own up to the fact that they are being lazy.

WHAT I DO:

1. **Draw** two trains on the board, labeling the top one, with smoke coming out of the smokestack, the E-Train and the bottom one the L-Train. The L-Train doesn't have any smoke. Example:

2. **Explain** that the E stands for the word *effort*. It takes effort to get work done and be successful.

- In front of the E-Train **make a bullet point** followed by the word *effort*.

- **Explain** that another good e-word is *energy*. It takes energy to get work done.
- Below the word *effort* **make a bullet point** followed by the word *energy*.

- **Explain** that the E can also stand for the word *engage*. You have to engage or connect with your work—be curious—to make it yours. Add this in a bullet point.

Tip

You may need to define the word *engage*. Explain that it is the opposite of being passive and indifferent.

- **Explain** that you can also think of the E-Train as the Express Train. Being on the express train, using effort, energy, and engagement will get you to your goals faster. Example:

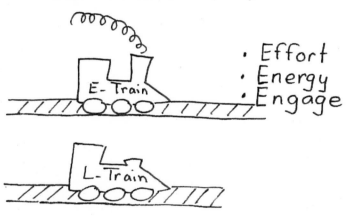

3. **Ask:** what do you think the L stands for? (Let participants provide answers. They usually get the first two quickly.)

- **Answer:** Lazy is one choice.

- In front of the L-Train, **make a bullet point** followed by the word *lazy*.

- **The second answer:** Loser is often chosen by teenagers.

- In front of the L-Train, **make a bullet point** followed by the word *loser*.

- **The third answer:** Laid-back might be used by the young adult hanging out in a coffee shop.

Tip

If you don't want to use the word "lazy" to name the L-Train, you might find it helpful to rename it the "Later Train." It is appropriate for the procrastinators who say, "I'll do it later." This is for those who are in the mode of, "I don't want to do it." They choose to play or let someone else do the work.

More About Lazy

Those with executive functioning deficits and learning disabilities often are labeled *lazy* because their output, like getting homework done, may not meet the expectations of those around them. Let me be perfectly clear that I do *not* consider them to be lazy. I wish everyone had the opportunity, as I've had, to work hour after hour next to children struggling to learn to read or to put down their thoughts on paper. No one works harder than these children, striving, step-by-step to develop competence while having a brain that makes it very difficult. These children are my heros.

In *Mindset*, Carol Dweck speaks about effort and those with learning disabilities, stating: "Often for them it is not sheer effort that works but finding the right strategy."

•In front of the L-Train, **make a bullet point** followed by the word *laid-back*. Example:

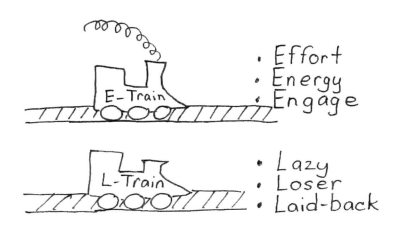

4. **Say:** We all have a choice, every day—every minute, really—to be on either the E-Train or the L-Train.

5. **Draw** train tracks going off in three directions in front of the E-Train. Example:

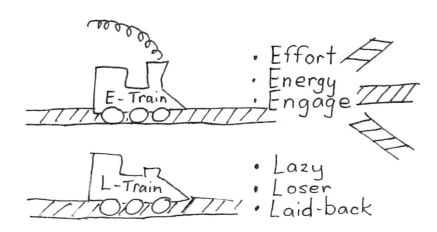

   •**Explain** that the thing about being on the E-Train is that your life will actually go somewhere. You have choices and possibilities.

6. **Explain** that all of us have moments of choosing to be on the L-Train. However, the problem with spending too much time on the L-Train is that it doesn't go anywhere.

7. **Draw** a wall in front of the L-Train, over the words *lazy, loser,* and *laid-back*. Example:

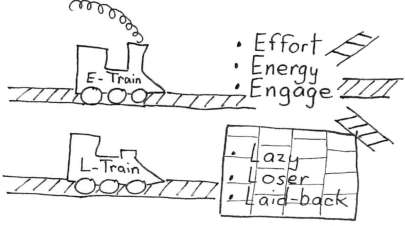

•Staying on the L-Train will limit your life's choices.

• It's difficult to make a good living if you are lazy, choosing to play more than work.

8. **Draw** a track connecting the L-Train to the E-Train along with a stick figure on the L-Train track. Example:

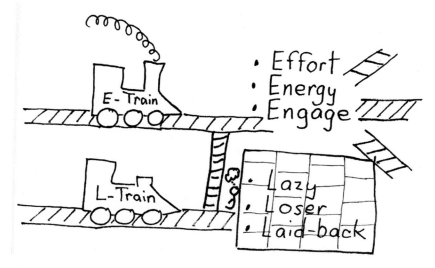

• **Explain** how a sixth grade student changed the trains story forever when he added a track connecting the L-Train to the E-Train. He also drew a little person sitting in front of the wall on the L-Train track. When asked why he drew that new track he said, "Well, that's how you get off the L-Train and onto the E-Train." But of course! The little person he drew was making the choice to get on the E-Train.

9. **Recap** these points:

    • Being successful takes effort, energy, and engagement.

    • We have the power to choose what to do with our time.

ACTIVITY:
Ask participants to draw on page 15 about the two trains of life.

Unit 2:
The First Truth
of Time

Out of Sight, Out of Mind

Key Points

1. The time-challenged do what is in sight.

2. The invisible nature of time causes a problem for the time-challenged brain.

3. Use external time supports to stay aware of time and of what needs to be done.

This unit provides the rationale for why the time-challenged need to use certain kinds of strategies to support their brain. It explains that their time challenges are the result of both how their brain works and the nature of time itself.

The time-challenged tend to be visual thinkers who are drawn to focus on what is immediately in front of them. They live in the now. It is as if future time doesn't exist. They respond to what comes into their field of view.

The abstract invisible nature of time is nearly impossible for the time-challenged to understand because they can't see time and their brain lacks an internal sense of the passing of time.

Since their brain lacks time awareness, the solution is to use specific external tools and strategies to make time concrete and visible. The focus of this unit is a discussion of six different external tools that effectively help the time-challenged to be on time and get things done.

MATERIALS NEEDED:

- Dry erase board, markers, and eraser
- For each participant (parents included) a copy of the *Seeing My Time* workbook
- Sharp pencils with erasers
- 3 x 5 cards

- Small analog clock
- Small digital clock
- Digital timers (Available through my website: www.ExecutiveFunctioningSuccess.com)
- Sample two-page Month Calendar
- A My Day Sheet (In the appendix)
- A Week Sheet (In the appendix)
- Any size box with a lid

The First Truth of Time:

Out of Sight, Out of Mind

Page 17:
Out of Sight, Out of Mind

To teach time management to the time-challenged brain, you have to make abstract time concrete and visible.

WHAT I DO:

1. **Direct** participants to page 17.

2. **Explain** that "Out of sight, out of mind" is an old expression that is very significant for the time-challenged person. Remembering these words is the first step required to change time-management behavior. It will become a key to solving problems.

3. **Ask** everyone to hold their hands together, like a telescope, in front of one open eye (closing the other), imagining that they are looking through a video camera eyepiece. (Model this for them.) **Ask** them to pan the room looking only through their "video camera."

   (Allow a few seconds for this activity.) **Tell** them: Thank you. You may put down your camera.

4. **Ask:** Did you notice that you could only see a small field of view? **Explain** that for the time-challenged, what is in that small field of view is the only thing you really pay attention to. In other words, if you aren't looking at something, you tend not to think about it. It is as if it doesn't exist.

5. **Explain** that it is easy to end up forgetting to do the things that we don't see, like folding clothes that are in the dryer, or doing homework that is in the backpack on the floor next to the back door.

6. **Direct** participants to page 17 and ask them to please draw what the phrase "Out of sight, out of mind" means to them. Have participants describe their drawings.

7. **Demonstrate or discuss** why the nature of time causes problems for the time-challenged.

   The following skit is valuable to use with adolescents and parents. It is a fun way to point out that time is abstract and

Key Point

Abstract time needs to be made concrete and visible.

invisible, and it introduces why the time-challenged have to use external tools to stay grounded in time.

If you are working just with adults, you can simply talk about how time is abstract and invisible.

MATERIALS NEEDED:

•Any size box with a lid

ACTIVITY:

1. **Ask:** Have you ever taken a short cut to save time? Like cutting across the grass instead of staying on the sidewalk? (They'll nod yes.)

2. **Pick up** the box with a lid.

3. **Say:** I too have taken shortcuts, and all of my saved time is here in this box.

4. **Ask** the students to cup their hands together as if they are going to drink water out of a stream.

5. **Say:** I am going to put all of my saved time in your hands. Be really careful with it because it is extremely valuable stuff—we only get so much in our lifetime. When it is in your hands, I want you to explain what you see when you look at my saved time held in your hands.

   Act this out with some drama for effect. Carefully lift the lid on the box and snatch your saved time as if you are catching a fly. Make a show of putting the saved time in the students' hands. They will be looking at you like you're a little nuts, but it makes the session fun and gives a strong impression.

6. When the student comes up with the correct answer, "I don't see anything," **exclaim:** Yes! That is the problem with time, we can't see it. It is invisible, and since we know that our brain only wants to do what is right in front of it, we don't even think about time!

   Some of the more creative types will say things like, "I see puffy clouds and swirling colors." They are describing what they visualize in their mind, not what they see in their hand!

7. **To finish** the drama, scoop up your saved time from their open hands and say thank you. Put your time back in your box, explaining that someday you are going to need it. (Remember, a little humor goes a long way in building relationships with your clients.)

8. **Explain** that since we can't actually see time, we have to use external tools that support our brain in order to remember to get things done. The next page in the workbook is about what are called Tools for Time Management.

Page 18:
Tools for Time Management

The time-challenged must use external supports in order to manage their time to reach goals. Using specific tools externalizes the executive skills that their brain lacks internally.

This page will explain six different external tools to use. After each tool is introduced, the participants are asked to reflect and decide how or where or when they could use each tool to help them with their time management. Time is allowed after each reflection to share their thoughts. This opens the opportunity for discussion and problem solving as well as suggesting options the participants may not have thought of themselves.

MATERIALS NEEDED:

- Small analog clock
- Small digital clock
- Digital timers (available through my website: www.ExecutiveFunctioningSuccess.com)
- Sample two-page Month Calendar
- A My Day Sheet (In the appendix)
- Dry erase board on an easel

Analog Clocks

Believe it or not, the kind of clock used is important for the visually-oriented, time-challenged brain. The ubiquitous digital clock creates a problem for this brain because it only shows one aspect of time—the present. It is useful for knowing what time it is, but not for planning ahead in order to be on time. Analog clocks are more effective for the time-challenged because they provide a more complete picture of time—the past, the present, and the future.

For the time-challenged, a clock needs to be directly within sight and easily visible, or it is useless. I tell the story of the day that I discovered the Internet. It was my daughter's first day of middle school. After lunch I thought I'd take a few minutes to check out this web world the kids were always talking about. Well, the phone rang. It was my daughter. "Mom! Where are you? School's been out for twenty minutes, and you have the car pool!"

Oops . . . I'd just spent over three hours on the Internet! I had a large analog clock on the wall above the computer screen. Why didn't that help me?

Key Point
Use external tools to support a time-challenged brain.

Key Points
1. Digital clocks only show one aspect of time—the present.

2. Analog clocks, or face clocks, show three aspects of time—the present, the past, and the future.

I never looked up from the screen! Out of sight, out of mind. So before I left the house to pick her up, I grabbed a little analog clock and set it right in front of my computer screen where it still sits years and years later.

WHAT I DO:

1. **Hold up** a digital clock and **ask:** What aspect of time does a digital clock show us?

2. **The Answer:** The digital clock only shows us one aspect of time, the present. **Explain** that it is useful for knowing what time it is, right now.

3. **Hold up** an analog clock and tell them that this kind of clock, an analog clock, shows three aspects of time. **Ask:** What are they?

4. **The correct answer** is that analog clocks, in addition to showing the present, show us the past (How long have I been here?) and the future (How long is it before I have to leave to get to soccer on time?).

5. **Ask:** Where in your world do you need an analog clock so you don't forget about time passing? Lead the brainstorming discussion to include at least few of these answers:

   - Next to computers
   - Next to my bed
   - Where I do homework or paperwork
   - On my desk
   - Where I put on my makeup
   - In the shower
   - Next to the TV
   - On my wrist

A Story About Watches

The time-challenged are very resistant to wearing watches. When I was younger, I felt like a watch restricted my spontaneity. I was a free spirit—living in the now—not tied down by a watch. I'd been married six months when my husband told me, "If you ask me what time it is one more time, I'm getting a divorce."

He sounded serious. So, did I go out and get a watch? No. I got the cool new technology of the time—a lovely, slim electronic calculator that had a clock function. Now I could find out what time it was. But did it help me get to the bus on time? No. Why? Because it was

Tip

A shower clock? An analog clock in the shower can be critical for some of us who can stand there until the water runs cold. I gave one to my son when he moved into his first apartment. "Thanks, Mom! I'd never get to class without it." You can find a shower clock on a rope through my website under Cool Tools: www.Executive FunctioningSuccess.com.

Tip

When I ask people why they don't wear a watch, they usually say, "I don't need one. I've got my cell phone." I point out that a cell phone is *not* a watch. A cell phone is a phone first, and is kept out of sight in pockets or bags.

The solution? Get a cool watch, because wearing a watch is a fashion statement for many people. I encourage clients to search out a watch that they really *want* to wear. Of course, it should not be a digital watch—it needs to be analog.

85

kept in a pocket or purse and was out of sight and thus time was out of mind.

ACTIVITY:

Tell participants to write, on page 18, where they need analog clocks. **Share** responses.

Digital Timers

While I am not a fan of digital clocks, I am a huge fan of digital—not wind-up—timers. Timers alert the time-challenged to the passage of time. They can be used in several ways.

The time-challenged are often guilty of hyper-focus, unable to transition away from a task or activity that they find engaging. So, an annoying, repetitive digital timer alarm penetrates their brain and alerts them to the need to transition to something else.

Timers can be used as a warning bell to begin transitions such as getting ready to leave the house. By setting one for a limited period of time, they can be used as motivators to begin work on tasks that are unpleasant. They can also be set for limiting break times.

They can be used to time how long a task takes, which is critical for the time-challenged since they can't internally estimate how long something will take. This helps with the development of metacognition connected to time.

A vibrating timer can be useful in settings where noise is distracting to others. It can be used to monitor focus in work or classroom settings. When it goes off, it is a reminder to pause and notice if you are actually doing what you set out to do or if you have been distracted.

WHAT I DO:

1. **Pick up** a timer and explain that the digital timer can be a best friend of the time-challenged.

2. **Ask** participants if, when they are really focused, such as when playing a video game, does the little ding of a wind-up timer cause them to stop playing? (Most readily admit that it wouldn't.)

3. **Set the timer** for one second. **Start the timer** and let it beep for a while. **Ask** if this annoying beep would penetrate their brain and remind them that it is time to get ready for soccer? (Most agree that it would.)

Tip

Small analog clocks can actually be hard to find. I buy them in bulk and sell them to interested clients. If you can't find one easily, check out my website for one option under Cool Tools at www.ExecutiveFunctioningSuccess.com.

Key Point

Digital timers are useful for transitions, staying on task, reminders, motivation, and learning to estimate time.

Tip

Some watches and phones have timer functions that are useful during the school or work day.

There are a number of timer applications, or widgets, that are useful on the computer. Look online or ask someone under the age of twenty-five.

Tip

I set my vibrating timer for ten-minute intervals. When it goes off, I pause to think if I'm on task or if I am doing something else, like roaming around a website.

4. **Explain** the following about how timers are useful for transitions:

- A digital timer's persistent beeping can break into the hyper-focus that is symptomatic of some people: an adolescent playing a video game, for instance.

- It's helpful to place it across a room so you have to get up to turn it off.

- This break in focus allows for metacognition to kick in and remind the time-challenged that it is time to quit the game and to transition to another task, such as homework or getting ready to leave for a meeting.

- Get a cook's timer that goes around your neck and use it to remind you to get ready to leave the house, allowing fifteen to twenty minutes to actually get out the door with all the necessary items. (A timer on a rope is featured on my website under Cool Tools.)

5. **Explain** the following about how timers can be used to monitor focus, useful for those with ADHD tendencies.

- When it goes off, pause and check in with yourself to see if you are actually doing what you are supposed to be doing.

- An interval timer, like those used by athletes in training, is handy because it can be set in a quieter vibrating mode. This is useful in office settings where a louder timer would be distracting to coworkers.

6. **Explain** how the digital timer also helps us remember to do things that are out of sight and out of mind, like change the laundry from the washer to the dryer or take medications.

7. **Explain** how a timer can be useful for motivation:

- If a task is loathsome or large, break it into smaller chunks. Set the timer for a period of time and then take a break when it goes off. (Of course, remember to set it again for five minutes to remind you to get back to the task if you need to!)

A Timer Story
One client started to use a timer to remember to add money to the parking meter. Her number of parking tickets went down!

Tip
Many clients have found that big projects, like cleaning closets, actually get done by using a timer. Set the timer and work just fifteen minutes, and then quit and move on to other things that need to be done. Little by little, the closet gets cleaned because, realistically, few of us have large blocks of time free for big projects, so we just don't start.

8. **Explain** how digital timers can be used to learn how to estimate time:

- The time-challenged are often unrealistic about how long it takes to do something.

- Timing activities is critical to developing the ability to estimate how long something will take to do.

A Story About Estimating Time

It takes practice and metacognition to become good at estimating time. When I was first trying to figure out my time challenges, I actually timed everything I did for a week just to see where my time was going, and then I made a chart. I was amazed and horrified at how completely wrong my time estimates were. It was no wonder I was always late and stressed.

ACTIVITY:

Tell participants to write, on page 18, when they could use a digital timer. **Share** responses.

Month Calendars

Like the analog clock, the Month Calendar provides a critical big picture of time: the past, the present, and the future. Families need one master calendar that includes everyone's commitments. It is important to stress that to be useful, a calendar needs to be kept in sight, readily visible; otherwise things get forgotten because they're "out of sight, out of mind."

WHAT I DO:

Explain the following points about Month Calendars:

- Everyone needs at least one Month Calendar in their life.

- Students need an assignment book/planner that has a month view versus a week view. (The week view is not useful because once you turn the page, every reminder on that week is suddenly out of sight and out of mind.)

- It is especially useful for college students to have a series of calendar months, representing the quarter or semester, in view above their desks. If exams and paper due dates are written down, they can see the future of the term and balance getting work done.

A Calendar Story

Where you hang a calendar is important if it is going to be useful. I had a client who consistently forgot to bring her son to his tutoring sessions. Visiting her home one day, I was not surprised to see that the family calendar, with her appointments, was kept on the *back* of the kitchen door and was out of sight 99 percent of the time. Remember, out of sight, out of mind.

Tip

Having your month calendar in sight or easily accessible is important. My personal solution is to carry around a planner with a monthly calendar that has a two-page spread. It has adequate space to pencil in both my business and home appointments. If there is a change in my schedule, I erase it—very easy—no scrolling or typing. I refer to it when I do my weekly planning. Our family calendar is on the wall next to the refrigerator.

• Families need a calendar that holds everybody's important commitments. Post it where it is useful and in sight. Plan the time to sync everybody's calendars and limit conflicts.

• Electronic and web-based calendars are all the rage. However they have big drawbacks. Most of the time, they are out of sight. They give can you a tiny picture of the future and can be difficult for family members to access.

• In office settings, it is useful to have two computer screens: one dedicated to the time-management calendar and the other for the working applications. Without this option, some people print off their Month Calendars, but if there are changes, they have to print off the updated versions.

ACTIVITY:

Tell participants to write, on page 18, where they need monthly calendars. **Share** responses.

The Daily Plan

Since the time-challenged want to do what is in front of them, it is critical to have a daily list of goals and commitments kept in sight.

WHAT I DO:

1. **Explain** that with a brain that focuses only on what it sees, it is critical to have a plan for the day kept in sight.

2. **Explain** that a plan for the day can be kept in sight in different ways:

    • It can be a sheet of paper on a clipboard.

    • It can be clipped to the front of a planner or binder.

    • It can be a small dry erase board on a desk or a larger dry erase board on a wall or easel.

3. **Explain** that using electronic devices for daily plans are problematic because we use our phones and computers for other applications. So the day plan is often out of sight and mind. Solutions include:

    • Printing off a daily schedule and clipping it to something in sight

- Using two screens, keeping the daily schedule open on one screen and using applications on the second screen

- Wrapping a large sticky note around a cell phone as a to-do reminder, since the phone is often used and thus in sight

ACTIVITY:

Tell participants to write, on page 18, where they need to keep their day plan so it will be in sight. **Share** responses.

Weekly Plans

Planning for the whole week is the base for good daily planning and time management in general. Like the day plan, the weekly plans need to be readily accessible if not immediately in sight.

WHAT I DO:

Say: In the next session we will be covering the important step of weekly planning. Keeping your weekly plan very close to your day plan is important since it is the basis for daily planning.

ACTIVITY:

Tell participants to write, on page 18, where they need to keep their weekly plans so that they will be in sight. **Share** responses.

The Dry Erase Board on an Easel

Well-placed dry erase boards are terrific tools for the time-challenged. They can be used for both daily scheduling and for planning the steps needed to complete complex projects. In my home we use small boards for things like grocery lists, phone messages, and communication between family members.

In my office I have a 3´ x 5´ wall-mounted board that helps me keep moving on all of my multiple projects. Many of my clients have adopted one of my favorite tools: a large dry erase board on an easel. Placed in a high-traffic area, it effectively keeps personal and family goals in sight so they get done.

WHAT I DO:

1. **Explain** that many families and individuals have reported great success with having a dry erase board on an easel in their homes. It is placed where everyone will repeatedly have to look at it as each day or weekend progresses. (Assure folks that it folds up easily for nights when you have company.)

Tip
I clip my Week of Actions plan to the outside of my planner, just underneath the My Day Sheet. That makes it easy for me to reference what still needs to be done as I move through the week.

A Dry Erase Board Story
After a few sessions, a seventh-grade girl reported that the dry erase board was working well. It was keeping her mother off her back.

2. **Explain** the following points as you draw a sample on the dry erase board. Example below:

- It is great for families because at a glance, everyone is aware of what the other family members have to do and want to do.

- Each family member gets a corner of the board for their own. (It is not a place for Mom to put down what she wants them to do.)

- Here is where they write to-do lists, just enough to actually get done in a day or two.

- Each person should also be planning for fun things to do, which also go on the board.

- Keeping these goals in sight enables everyone to remember to work on their goals and get them done. Example:

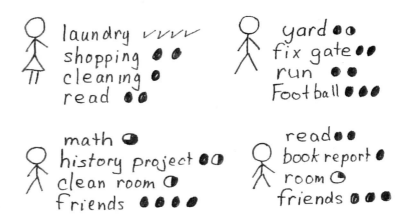

- It allows parents to be supportive rather than nagging.

If parents notice that their son hasn't started work on his school project, rather than saying, "If you don't get that homework done, you aren't going to Nathan's this afternoon," they can say, "I noticed on the dry erase board that you haven't finished working on your project. Is there something I can do to help you get started?"

The latter approach is much more supportive and less likely to get a defensive response.

(I actually act this out playing the role of the threatening mother. I can see the child physically tighten up as I speak. I ask the child how it feels to get this message. They respond that they don't like it. When I switch to the supportive language, the child relaxes and can verbalize that it feels better than the first approach.)

I then turn to the parents and suggest that when they see their child not working on homework, they should approach the problem by first asking themselves and the child, "Where is the confusion?" And then asking, "How can I help you get started?"

•The dry erase board also sets up opportunities for honest praise. "Hey, I noticed you finished your math homework. Good going!"

ACTIVITY:

Tell participants to write, on page 18, how they might use a dry erase board and where they would put it so that it's in sight. **Share** responses.

Page 19:
Such Is Life . . .

Many of the time-challenged neglect doing mundane tasks—grocery shopping, menu planning, laundry, housework, bill paying, taxes, etc.—because they "just don't have time" or "don't feel like it." Avoiding doing these kinds of things can create a more stressful life, always on the edge of crisis—no clean clothes, nothing for dinner, checks bouncing, late taxes, etc.

The time-challenged need to develop the metacognitive awareness to see that their time-management choices complicate their life. Choosing to do what needs to be done, on time, will actually lead to less stress. Fun and relaxation need to be planned for, after the responsibilities are handled.

WHAT I DO:

1. **Direct** participants to page 19.

2. **Choose** a participant to read aloud the words: *Such is life . . . Life requires doing things that you don't want to do—on time and to the best of your ability.*

3. **Say:** To be successful in life requires constantly doing things that you really would rather not do—some of it very mundane, like laundry, dishes, mowing the lawn, and homework.

   - Our lives just work better if we handle our responsibilities.

   - Life is less stressful when we keep on top of the things that have to be done.

   - Perhaps a primary purpose of our educational system should be to teach students to do quality work, on time, which gets them ready for their adult work life.

4. **Direct** participants to respond to the prompt: *What I need to do but don't really want to do.* **Share** responses.

Think About It

Many of us have a negative reaction to the word *responsibility*. Being responsible is somehow connected with work and being grown up—the opposite of a free, creative spirit.

Reframe the word *responsible* by breaking it apart into its components: *response* and *able*.

In this light, *responsible* really means that you are able to respond. You have choice. As the time-challenged develop their metacognitive connection to time, they are finally able to choose to be responsible and get their have-tos done.

Unit 3:
The Second Truth
of Time

Time Takes Up Space

Key Points

1. Think of time spatially.

2. Plan your week using a visual list of actions or goals.

3. Use a Week Sheet that shows the space of time you have available to reach those goals.

Focus on the Spatial Aspect of Time

This unit is what sets apart *The Sklar Process* from traditional study skills and time-management programs. Dr. Ellyn Arwood at the University of Portland changed my life when she emphasized the importance of thinking of time spatially. When I struggled to understand my visual time-challenged brain, she gave me the obscure advice to "go home and take care of yourself in time and space." First I figured out that I had to come up with a way to see invisible time. Then I had to come up with a way to externally represent the second key point—the Second Truth of Time—that time takes up space.

The Abstract Nature of Time Is the Problem

Once again it is the nature of time that causes the problem. Time can seem stretchable. If you are enjoying yourself and are very focused, it goes quickly. If you are doing something tedious, it seems to slow down. To complicate matters, the time-challenged can have some pretty strange ideas about how time works. They are very unrealistic about what they can get done in a set period of time.

Draw a Mind Map to See a Week's Plan

After introducing the concept that time takes up space, this unit presents strategies to use for time management, beginning with answering the question: where does your time go? The activity is to draw what takes up time and space in your week. It is a visual

Resource

For more about drawing a mind map, read *Mapping Inner Space: Learning and Teaching Visual Mapping* by Nancy Margulies.

95

format following the idea of specific roles in your life as outlined in Stephen Covey's *The Seven Habits of Highly Effective People*.

Once the roles and activities have been represented by icons, the participants then determine the time required for each specific activity or commitment. They are taught to visually represent time with filled-in circles. They create moveable flags for repetitive activities like homework, chores, and exercise.

Determine Available Time

When this picture of the week is completed, it is time to answer the second question: where is the space in the week to get things done? The second activity of the unit is filling in a form that shows the space of time in a week between 6:00 A.M. and 11:00 P.M. The goal is to block out all the commitments in order to see the empty spaces available.

When working with middle school and high school students, I provide an additional form that shows only the afternoon and evening, the time period after school, when they have choices. This gives an expanded view of each afternoon and evening hour, allowing more room to use the removable flags.

Use Removable Sticky Arrows

Once the empty spaces are delineated, removable sticky arrows are used to plan the space to do the tasks. Questions are asked like: Where can I fit in my math homework? My history? Paying bills? Laundry? Weekly planning?

This process gives the time-challenged a clear visual picture of where their time goes in a week and where they have the space to get necessary work done.

Some clients will quickly see that they live overbooked lives, which is one source of stress. Concretely seeing this allows them to pause, reflect, and think about their choices. Some choose to simplify their lives so they have more time and space to slow down. At a minimum they stop beating themselves up for not getting everything done. You can't do it all. They learn to say no to people so they don't add to their commitments. They see the need to delegate and get help.

For some, the picture of the space in their week is enlightening because while they feel harried, they actually do have the space to get homework, etc., done if they choose to do it.

MATERIALS NEEDED:

- Dry erase board, markers, and eraser
- For each participant (parents included) a copy of the *Seeing My Time* workbook
- Sharp pencils with erasers
- 3 x 5 cards
- Sticky arrow flags or other sticky removable products approximately 1/4 inch wide, like those shown on my website under Cool Tools or found where you buy sticky notes. (Another option is to cut up bigger sticky notes into strips, but these are not as durable.)
- For all adults, a take-home copy of the Week Sheet that begins at 6:00 A.M. (In the appendix)
- For students, a copy of the Afternoon Week Sheet that shows seven days, afternoons only (In the appendix)

Page 21:
Time Takes Up Space

The time-challenged need to visually see where their time goes and the amount of time each activity takes.

WHAT I DO:

1. **Direct** participants to page 21.

2. **Choose** someone to read aloud the headings: *The Second Truth of Time: Time Takes Up Space. Time does NOT s-t-r-e-t-c-h so you can do more.*

3. **Say:** Because you can't see time, you tend to think of time as sort of stretchable. When you're having fun, time seems to go quickly. When you're doing something you don't want to do, like waiting for your mom to get out of the grocery store while you're sitting in the car, the time really slows down. But in truth, it just keeps going at the same speed. Time is not like a balloon that stretches to allow you to do more things in a given space. Think of time as more like a rigid box with a lid. You can only get so much into a box with a lid.

ACTIVITY:

1. **Invite** everyone to draw what they see in their mind when you say: "Time takes up space." (One of my favorite drawings was based on words. A sixth-grader wrote: "An hour is an hour, not an HHHOOOOOUUUURRRRR.")

2. **Share** responses.

A Time Story

Not only does time not stretch, it doesn't stop for us. It just keeps on going. This may seem obvious, but I had an adult give this as his key point. He confessed to thinking that when he checked out on a Saturday to play games on the computer, time would magically pause and wait for him. He thought that once he was done playing, he'd be able to begin the day all over again, as if those hours of play hadn't happened.

Seeing What Takes Up the
Space of My Time

Page 22:
Seeing What Takes Up the Space of My Time

This activity gives the participants a visual picture of where their time goes in a week. Unlike a linear list, this picture shows at glance what needs to be done in each sphere of your life. It provides a way to make sure that all parts of your life are getting the attention needed.

Rather than make a list of goals, I draw a mind map of my week, showing all the roles in my life that take up time in any given week. I put the paper in the landscape direction because it matches the orientation of our eyes and makes it easy to take in the week at quick glance.

If you are working with a family unit, focus on guiding the child through the process. Adults usually do fine on their own once shown an example.

Definition of Roles

Student Roles/Activities
Sports
Music or dance lessons
Scouts
Drama
Religious activities
Homework
Chores
Friends
Work
Personal time

Adult Roles/Activities
Household
Parenting
Earning money
Volunteering
Friends/extended family
Spouse/significant other
Religious activities
Exercise/hobbies

Since a picture is worth a thousand words, please look at the example of how I draw my week. Then take the time to draw your own upcoming week. Keep it and use it as a sample to show your clients. (Steven Covey uses the word *roles* to divide up the activities we do in a week. For instance an adult may be: a parent, an employee, a spouse, a volunteer, a son or daughter, and a friend. Keep the number of roles to a maximum of seven. The page should not be visually overwhelming.)

MATERIALS NEEDED:
- A sample drawing of your week to share with your clients. (It will give you credibility.)
- Optional: Create two sample posters, 11 x 14 inches each and laminate them. One should show the roles of a typical child and the other, roles for an adult. Without posters, you'll need to draw examples on the dry erase board. See examples below.

WHAT I DO:
1. **Say:** To plan your time, you have to know where it goes—what you do in a given week. You will do this by drawing a mind map of your typical week. It will show all the roles or activities you have that require time each week.

2. **Show or draw** an example of a mind map showing roles. Explain how instead of making a list, you've used little icon drawings to represent each of the roles. Tell them not to stress over the drawing. Keep it simple. It is not an art project. Just make simple iconic images for each of the roles or major activities in their life. Example of adult week:

Example of student week:

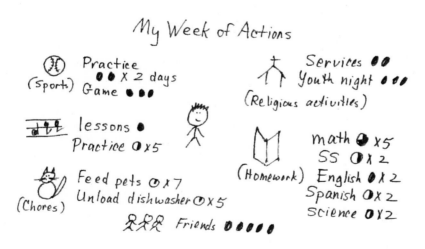

3. **Describe** typical student roles/activities: sports, lessons of various kinds, scouting, interest groups like choir or drama, religious activities, family time, chores, time spent with friends, and homework.

4. **Describe** typical adult roles such as being a parent, a spouse, or a friend. They may also be responsible for aging parents or

extended family, community volunteering, religious activity, domestic responsibilities, and being a wage earner.

5. **Tell** all participants to be sure to add a special icon for an activity that is really important for them to do, something that refreshes them, or is fun or relaxing. You need to plan to have fun in your life, just as you plan for work and responsibilities.

ACTIVITY:

1. **Direct** participants to turn to page 22.

Direct participants to turn to page 22.

2. **Tell** them to first draw themselves in the middle of the page. Then make a little drawing for each of the roles or activities that takes up time in their week. They should be simple symbols, like those used for clip art. Be sure that students draw a symbol for school. (Later in the process, they will add homework under the school symbol.)

3. **Say:** Now that you can see what takes up your time, you need to figure out how much time you spend on these activities each week. We need to be able to see the amount of space each activity takes up. In order to see the space, we are going to use circles to represent time on an analog clock.

4. **Demonstrate** on the dry erase board how a filled-in circle will represent one full hour. Half of a circle represents half an hour. Likewise one fourth of the circle equals fifteen minutes, and three quarters of a circle is forty-five minutes. Example:

Time circles represent a clock.

1 hour   30 min.   45 min.   15 min.   10 min.

5. **Direct** participants to list specific actions that need doing under each role. For adults this might be: How long will the doctor's appointment take? How long will grocery shopping take? How long does it take to walk the dog?

6. **Help** students determine how long they spend on activities like soccer. **Remind** them to allow time for getting dressed for practice, driving to practice, the actual practice or game,

Tip

This is an idea from Dr. Ellyn Arwood. She felt it was important for visual thinkers to see themselves connected to their actions. I agree with her. By drawing myself in the middle of my Week of Actions, I am taking ownership of my time and what I want to do.

and then driving home. How many times a week do they have practice?

Have them draw the circles for each of their activities over the span of one week. Do school last. Example:

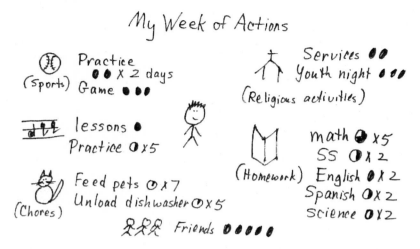

7. **For students:**

- **Direct** them to now list under the school icon all the subjects that require them to do homework.

- **Ask** them to estimate how long it takes them to finish assignments in each subject.

- **Draw** time circles next to each subject. Multiply their estimate by the number of nights in a week that they typically have each activity. (Students generally have little awareness of how long it takes to do assignments. This session's homework will be to time how long it actually takes to do homework assignments.)

Example detail for student homework:

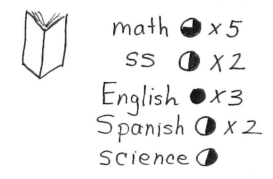

Page 23:
The Space in a Week

The time-challenged need to be able to concretely see the space of time in their week. This enables them to visualize when they will have the time and space to get things done.

MATERIALS NEEDED:

- A filled-in example of a Week Sheet
- Take-home copies of the full Week Sheet for each adult participant (In the appendix)
- Take-home copy of the Afternoon Week Sheet for each student (In the appendix)
- Take-home copy of the My Day Sheet for each adult (In the appendix)
- Removable sticky arrows
- Plastic sheet protector that opens in the front with easy access for the student's afternoon sheet

WHAT I DO:

1. **Direct** participants to page 23.

2. **Say:** This is a picture of the space of time in a whole week, if you got up at 6:00 A.M. and went to bed at 11:00 P.M. (Which is not recommended because that would give you seven hours of sleep—the minimum for adults. Adolescents should be getting between 8.5 and 9.5 hours of sleep per night.)

3. **Say:** Once you know what you have to do in a week, the next step is to figure out the space—or time—when you are going to get things done.

4. **Show** them a filled in example of a Week Sheet. Example:

Resource

Poor sleep habits are a major problem in our society. Our brain needs adequate sleep to have maximum executive functioning skills. Teens especially struggle because of inadequate sleep. Read *Snooze . . . or Lose! 10 "No-War" Ways to Improve our Teen's Sleep Habits* by Helene Emsellem.

Thursday	Friday	Saturday	Sunday
Date _____	Date 10/6	Date 10/7	Date 10/8
6:00	6:00	6:00	6:00
6:30	6:30	6:30	6:30
7:00	7:00	7:00	7:00
7:30 Leave	7:30 Leave	7:30	7:30
8:00 ↓	8:00 ↓	8:00	8:00
8:30 School	8:30 School	8:30	8:30
9:00	9:00	9:00 Leave	9:00
9:30	9:30	9:30 ↓	9:30
10:00	10:00	10:00 Soccer	10:00
10:30	10:30	10:30	10:30 Leave
11:00	11:00	11:00	11:00 Church
11:30	11:30	11:30	11:30

5. **Explain** that you only block out your commitments—those activities where you have to be somewhere such as:
- school
- work
- after-school lessons or activities
- sports practice and games
- organization meetings
- appointments
- religious activities

6. **Advise** them not to block out time for activities that they have to fit in and around their commitments. They will deal with those kinds of things in a few minutes. These would include:
- homework
- housework
- hobbies
- chores
- independent exercise
- errands
- phone calls
- emails

ACTIVITY:

If you are working with a family group, focus your attention on guiding the student through this activity. The parent can work independently. You will have to interrupt the parent to get clarification on the child's activities, since he or she rarely has a sense of the time their activities take.

Tip

For students who are tightly booked, stress that they *really* need to have good time-management skills in order to be successful students.

WHAT I DO:

1. **Direct** participants to page 23, to the column for Monday.

2. **Ask:** What time do you have to leave the house in order to be at school or work on time? **Explain** that there is no such thing as the perfect form, so they will have to pick the line just before their leaving time. On the appropriate line, write *school* or *work*.

3. **Ask:** On a Monday, what time do you walk in the door at home after school or work? Write *home* on that line. **Draw** a line from the leaving home time to the getting home time, essentially blocking out the day where there is little free choice about what you get done.

4. **Say:** It is critical to block out time for sleep because the time-challenged tend to just keep going and going, and end up not getting enough sleep.

   • Adults need between seven and eight hours a night.

   • Adolescents need between eight and a half and nine and a half hours a night. **Help** them calculate a bed time that would enable them to get adequate sleep each night.

   • **Tell** them to write *sleep* at the time they will need to turn out the lights to get enough sleep.

5. **Proceed** to fill out the entire week. Students may have different school start and ending times depending on the day. They may also have after-school activities that need to be accounted for before they actually get home.

6. **Ask:** Looking at your week, what do you notice about your time? Some will see that they have little free time, while others will be impressed by the amount of empty space in their week.

7. **For students:** Introduce the Afternoon Week Sheet which shows the space of time, after school, during which they can choose to do things.(See the appendix.) Example:

Tip

Some students are amazed to see that they actually have a fair amount of free time. They felt pressured, but it was because they were choosing to do fun activities for large chunks of time, leaving homework until they were squeezing it in at the end of the day before going to sleep.

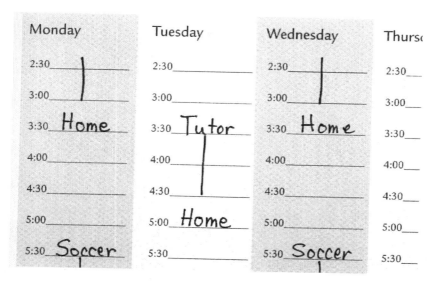

If you have enough session time, have students complete this form just as they did on the whole week form. If time is short, have them fill it out at home and bring it back to the next session.

NOTE: This may be as far as you get in this session. If so, go to the checkout on page 26.

Over-Scheduling

Over-scheduling is a source of stress for many children and adults. Some people have very full lives—too full. They will look down at their filled-in Week Sheet and say, "I don't have any free time." Yes. That is their choice. Let them know that it is also a choice to try not to do so much in a week.

Looking at this form helped me learn to say no to people who wanted me to volunteer to do things. I could easily say, "Thanks for asking, but there is no time in my week for any more commitments."

ACTIVITY:

I use removable arrows for repetitive tasks that need to get done. Putting tasks on removable arrows keeps them in sight and in mind, which is useful for tasks that tend to be put off—homework, laundry, or menu planning. Removable arrows also help you see where a task will fit into your day. They are another way of seeing the spatial aspect of time. If a task isn't completed, the arrow is moved to another open space on another day. This way the task stays in sight.

MATERIALS NEEDED:

- A filled-in example of a Week Sheet from the previous activity
- Sticky arrow flags or other sticky removable products approximately 1/4 inch wide

WHAT I DO:

1. **Say:** With your Week of Actions you have figured out what takes up your time. With the Week Sheet you put down all your commitments, looking for the open spaces in your week. Now you are going to use removable flags to help you find the time to do the tasks and goals for the week.

2. **Direct** participants back to page 22, their mind map of their week with the drawings of their roles and activities for the week. Give them each some arrow flags.

3. **Ask** them to choose repetitive tasks that need to happen this week. Have them write the action down on the flag along with a time circle that estimates the amount of time they will need to finish the task.

   - Adults will put down tasks like paying bills, laundry, and family planning time.

   - Students will make flags for each of their homework subjects, which they will soon be placing on their Afternoon Week Sheet. If they have homework in math four nights a week, they will need to make four flags labeled Math. Be sure to have them draw time circles to represent the time and space they need to be able to do the work.

4. **Direct** participants back to page 23 (or the student Afternoon Week Sheet). Tell them to place the arrow flags in the empty spaces when they can get the work done. (Students will need to find room for all their homework flags.) Example:

Tip

When I started out to get control of my time management, I had a flag for *everything* I did in a week. Now, I only use them for tasks that I'm avoiding and need to keep front and center in order to work on them. I used a lot of flags while writing my books!

A Story of Change

After looking at his afternoon and evening homework schedule, a sophomore in high school made a dramatic change. The following week, he reported to me that he was now using class time and study hall to get most of his assignments done at school. That way he had more free time at home. When he said this, I saw his father's jaw drop in amazement!

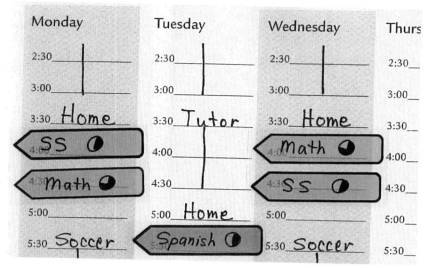

5. **Summarize** that planning your week is a critical task for good time management.

   • Time needs to be set aside to do weekly planning.

   • It is recommended that a maximum of thirty minutes a week be set aside for planning, usually on a weekend day.

   • If families do their individual planning while sitting down together, they will be able to coordinate plans and avoid the conflicts that arise from lack of communication about plans and needs.

6. **Explain** to students that they only need to fill out the space of the Week Sheet once a term or whenever after-school activities change. They can store their sheet in a sheet protector and put the flags on the top so they can be moved around as needed. Provide a sheet protector to the students so they have a durable tool ready to use.

7. **Ask** participants where they should keep their Week Sheets.

   • For students, discuss options, stressing that the location must be somewhere in sight where homework is done in order for this to be a useful strategy.

   • Adults may keep theirs clipped under their day plans, to be used as reference for daily planning.

8. **Send** participants home with Week Sheets (Afternoon Week Sheets for students) and My Day Sheets.

9. **Briefly** show them the My Day Sheet, (found on page 65 in the *Course Notes*) pointing out that in addition to showing the space of the day, the icons group daily actions: phone calls, letters, emails, and errands. The box on the lower right is working-memory support, where you write things you need to remember to do. Example:

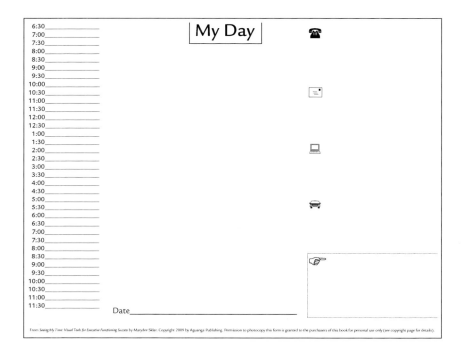

Students rarely need this form, although both of my children when they were in high school would ask me for "that form you use" when planning heavy homework loads on the weekends.

Page 24:
Summary of Weekly Planning

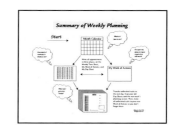

The weekly planning process is critical for the time-challenged. They need to sit down and see the coming week in order to feel grounded. It lowers stress and conflicts, so I encourage clients to set aside thirty minutes on Sundays for family planning. With this base it takes less than five minutes each day to write up a plan for the day.

WHAT I DO:

1. **Direct** participants to page 24.

2. **Explain** that this page is a visual summary of how to plan your week.

3. **Summarize** the steps:

   • You begin with your Month Calendar with its appointments and commitments.

   • Block out your commitments on the Week Sheet.

   • Draw your mind map showing your Week of Actions for the coming week, listing goals and commitments.

   • Every day, fill in a My Day Sheet, referring back to both the Week Sheet and the mind map for the week.

   • Keep all your My Day Sheets until the next weekly planning time. Transfer any unfinished tasks to your new mind map of the week.

4. **Emphasize** the following:

   • This should be done once a week.

   • Pick a day and time, and be consistent.

5. **Discuss** what would be a good time for your clients to do their planning.

6. **Summarize** the steps:

Tip

I made a master copy of my Week of Actions, showing myself in the middle surrounded by icons for all my roles and activities. I photocopy stacks of them, front and back, to have ready for my weekly planning when I fill in the lists of things that need doing.

Tip

Setting aside time for weekly planning is critical for the time-challenged, and they have difficulty creating the habit. I send weekly email reminders to my clients about their sessions. To support their planning, I will sometimes include a question like, "How's the planning going?" Clients have appreciated this simple nudge in the early weeks of the program.

- Begin with your Monthly Calendar with its appointments and commitments.

- Block out your commitments on the Week Sheet.

- Draw your mind map of the coming week, listing goals and commitments.

- Every day fill in a My Day Sheet, referring back to both the Week Sheet and the mind map for the week, My Week of Actions.

- Keep all your My Day Sheets until the next weekly planning time. Transfer any unfinished tasks to your new mind map of the week.

Page 25:
Whatever Needs to Get Done— Be Sure to Keep It in Sight

The time-challenged often ignore what they need to do by hiding the task—out of sight, out of mind. They will bury bills, tax forms, and assignments in piles so they can forget about them. They will close doors on messy rooms and closets. This page is a pause for participants to acknowledge what they need to keep in sight so they will do it.

WHAT I DO:

Direct participants to page 25.

ACTIVITY:

1. **Ask** one of the participants to read aloud the heading and subheading on page 25.

2. **Explain** that people often avoid doing unpleasant tasks because they forget about them by conveniently keeping the task out of sight and thus out of mind.

3. **Direct** participants to answer the question on page 25: What do I need to keep in sight?

4. **Share** responses.

Unit 4: Meeting Due Dates

The time-challenged are notorious for putting things off until the last minute and missing deadlines. Their executive functioning deficits in the areas of planning, prioritization, time management, and organization thwart the best of their intentions to get assignments and projects done on time with minimal stress and drama.

The problem is once again complicated by their lack of awareness of the passage of time and their inability to see the space of time in the future. The solution is to use the strategies of Unit 3 that make time visible and concrete, and to add a new skill set of being able to see the steps required to complete a project.

For the sake of instruction, the workbook provide sample assignments relevant to middle and high school students. Adults who work through the activities are able to interpret how they might use the same strategies in their own work or home life.

This unit teaches the following:

- Every project needs a plan before you begin.
- Understand the scope of a project by drawing out the directions and expectations for each step.
- Begin planning a project on the day you get the assignment.
- Plan by starting with the end result and going backwards to the starting point.
- Determine the space of time needed for each step, and show it using filled-in time circles.
- Find the space of time to do the steps by using sticky notes on a Month Calendar, beginning with the due date and working backwards.

MATERIALS NEEDED:

- Dry erase board, markers, and eraser
- For each participant (parents included) a copy of the *Seeing My Time* workbook
- Sharp pencils with erasers
- 3 x 5 cards
- Highlighter marker for each participant
- Pads of small sticky notes: approximately 2″ x 1-1/2″

Page 27:
Meeting Due Dates

WHAT I DO:

1. **Direct** participants to page 27. Choose someone to read aloud the words: *A goal without a plan is just a wish*.

2. **Say:** Saying that we are going to reach a goal is easy. Actually reaching a goal is something else altogether. Those people who seem to be able to do lots of amazing things in their life make plans. Then they work on the steps of their plans so that, little by little, they achieve their goal.

ACTIVITY:

1. **Invite** everyone to draw or write a personal goal that needs a plan.

2. **Briefly** share answers.

Page 28:
Getting Projects Done on Time

The purpose of this page is to acknowledge how both our choices and external events get in the way of finishing projects on time.

This is also the page where it is good to open discussion of the p-word: procrastination. The time-challenged usually have some strong negative feelings connected to that word. It was most likely their first five-syllable word, and they have worn the label of procrastinator for many years.

WHAT I DO:

1. **Direct** participants to page 28.

2. **Say:** It is challenging to get projects done on time. On the next page, we are going to begin using strategies that will help, but first we need to think about what gets in the way of doing projects.

ACTIVITY:

1. **Invite** participants to draw or write a response to the prompt: *Why is it hard to get projects done on time?*

2. **Briefly** share answers. Acknowledge that it is easy to be distracted by more pressing needs. It is also easy to get on the L-Train and avoid a project because you just don't want to do it.

3. **Explain** that people often say they don't start on projects until the last minute because they procrastinate—they are procrastinators.

4. **Ask** if any of the participants have ever been accused of procrastinating. (Odds are that heads will nod yes.) Explain that the strategies in the next few pages will help end procrastination on projects.

Tip

I tell parents that if you ask a child if they have any homework, they are apt to say no or that they got it done at school. The next question to immediately ask is, "Do you have any projects to work on?"

Ah . . . that is a different question. They squirm a little as they fess up to a report that is due next week.

In the mind of most students, homework only refers to that which is to be turned in within the next day or two.

Page 29:
Seeing My Assignment

There are at least two reasons why the time-challenged procrastinate. The first is that they don't have a clear picture of what a big project entails. They aren't always sure of what needs to be done. They often don't understand all of the steps. They don't know where to begin much less when to begin. The DVD brain needs a picture of the steps of a project.

The second reason is that procrastination may have an emotional component. When the teacher or employer first hands the time-challenged the project description, there is often a negative feeling. ("This is going to be so much work. What if I don't do it right?") Remember that the brain wants to protect us from painful and unpleasant emotions, so it pulls out the escape card.

The time-challenged often escape by putting the assignment out of sight, into a pile, promising themselves that they'll deal with it later since they've got lots of time before it is due. Not a good move. It was just put out of sight and thus . . . out of mind. This is the first step to the crisis of missing a deadline.

The following activity will provide a strategy to use whenever directions are given for an assignment or task that has multiple steps and is due at some point in the future versus due tomorrow.

WHAT I DO:

1. **Direct** participants to page 29.

2. **Explain** that the first step to ending project procrastination is to make sure you have a complete picture of what your teacher or boss wants you to do. You need to fully understand their expectations.

3. **Ask:** Have you ever turned in a project and gotten marked down because you left something out? (Heads will nod yes.) **Explain** that this strategy stops that from happening.

ACTIVITY:

1. **Direct** participants to the figure on the right of page 29, which represents the teacher or boss. The figure is explaining what he wants to be in the finished report or project: "You need to

Key Points

1. Having a complete picture of a project discourages procrastination.

2. Draw to understand and remember exactly what your teacher/boss wants you to do.

3. To fully understand the requirements of a project (and support working memory), read and respond to each sentence of the directions, clause by clause.

4. Do this drawing strategy on the day the project is assigned.

116

include a doughnut, a cylinder, and a hexagon."

2. **Direct** the participants to the figure on the left, which represents them with the project done. Their finished project needs to match the teacher's or employer's expectations. The figure has all the components asked for—plus a star. The star will be explained in a moment.

3. **Explain** that one reason people forget and leave things out is that we have limits to our working memory. It can only hold so much, which makes it easy to forget something when you are reading a long or complicated set of directions.

4. **Explain** that in the box on page 29 are the steps you need to take to build a complete picture of what you need to do for a project.

5. **Direct** participants to fill in the blanks with the answer you provide for each step. Read each step and provide the answer that is in bold print.

6. **Say:**

   - Draw what each clause or *sentence* tells you to do.

   - Stop at commas, *periods*, semicolons, colons, and the words *or* and *and*.

   - *Highlight* words after you draw them so you don't skip something by accident.

   - *Circle* important words or phrases: *should include*, *must include*, *also*, *has to have*, *for extra credit*, and *the minimum requirement*.

   - Put the deadlines on your *month calendar.*

Page 30:
Drawing My Assignment

By going over directions following the steps on page 27, the time-challenged are assured that they have a complete picture of what needs to be done. Using a highlighter pen guarantees that working memory is supported so no requirements are left out.

MATERIALS NEEDED:

- Dry erase board, markers, and eraser
- For each participant (parents included) a copy of the *Seeing My Time: Course Notes*
- Highlighter pen for each participant
- Foil stars (optional, but fun)

WHAT I DO:

1. **Direct** participants to page 30.

2. **Explain** that participants will now practice using the steps from page 29.

3. **Say:** The example assignment at the bottom of page 30 was excerpted from an actual two-page project description given to a sixth-grader. It is just a model project to use for this activity. You can use this strategy for any set of complicated directions. (If a student or adult has an actual project assignment in hand, use it instead of the sample project.)

ACTIVITY:

1. **Direct** participants to silently read the first bold-faced sentence in the assignment description. Tell them to use the highlighter to circle the word *and* in the sentence.

2. **Direct** one person to read aloud the part of that sentence that precedes the word *and*: *This project includes a written report on Egyptian pyramids.*

3. On the dry erase board **demonstrate** drawing the picture of what those words create in your mind. **Talk** as you draw: When I read those words, I see a piece of paper shown by a rectangle with words and a pyramid on it. Example:

4. **Ask** them to draw, in the left corner of the box, a picture of what those words mean to them.

5. **Direct** participants to use their highlighter pen to cover over only the words that they have just drawn: *This project includes a written report on Egyptian pyramids.*

6. **Direct** them to highlight the period at the end of the complete sentence—after the word *pyramids*.

7. **Direct** one person to read aloud the final clause of that first sentence: *and the construction of a model pyramid.*

8. **Explain** that you have just discovered that there are two very distinct parts to this project: a written report and a model of a pyramid.

9. On the right side of the dry erase board, **draw** a three-dimensional pyramid and write the word *model* next to it. Example:

10. **Direct** participants to draw a pyramid on page 30 and label it Model. Then direct them to highlight the words that they have just drawn.

11. **Direct** participants to silently read the second bold-faced sentence in the assignment description. Tell them to use the highlighter to cover over the period at the end of the sentence.

12. **Direct** one person to read aloud the bold-faced sentence: *The completed project will include a written report on pyramids.*

13. **Ask:** Do you already have that picture? **Answer:** Yes.

Explain that since they already have a picture of those words, they do not draw them again. Just highlight that sentence since that picture is done.

Poorly Written Directions Are Common

After pointing out the redundant sentence in the directions for the pyramid project, I explain that teachers work very hard and long hours. Sometimes the directions for projects are written at 10:30 at night, and no one ever proofreads them, so the assignment can be very confusing and poorly written. This causes students and parents lots of anxiety and frustration.

I've had master teachers wince as they admitted they'd passed out poorly written directions.

By drawing out an assignment, line by line, the day it's assigned, a student can find the points of confusion and ask the teacher for clarification the next day, something they can't do the evening before the project is due! If they get the teacher to clarify the instructions, the whole class will be thankful.

14. **Direct** participants to circle the words: *it should include*—noting that this is a warning that you don't want to forget any of the following points in your project. Remind students that leaving something out of your report means that your grade will be lowered.

15. **Direct** them to highlight the next comma and read aloud the words: *the building materials used*.

16. On the dry erase board **demonstrate** that the picture for these words goes under the drawing of the piece of paper since it goes with the report and not the model part of the project.

Explain that while some people draw building materials like rocks and sand, it is also recommended that they use a bullet point and write out the words *building materials* next to the drawing. This is a backup in case you can't remember later what your drawing represents! Example:

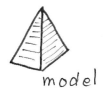

model

- building materials
- how built?

17. Once they have added building materials to their drawing, **ask** them to highlight that clause. **Proceed** through at least two more clauses, highlighting the commas, drawing the clause, including a bullet point description, and then highlighting when they've got it drawn.

18. **Check in** with participants to see if they've got the idea. If they do, stop the drawing, explaining that if this was a real assignment they'd go to the end.

19. **Direct** participants to look ahead to the sentence: *Any other information you find interesting may be included.* Have them circle this sentence.

20. **Explain** that these words are teacher-speak for "extra credit." This is what the star stood for back on page 29.

21. **Direct** participants back to page 29 and label the star Extra Credit. Before leaving page 30, explain that they will also need to record all due dates given in the assignment directions, writing them down on their Month Calendar.

Page 31:
Planning Backwards and Assigning Time

I came up with Planning Ahead by Planning Backwards when my then fifth-grade son came home with a report project on Sir Francis Drake due in one month. When I suggested that he start on it, he blew me off with the old line, "I've got lots of time. It's not due for a month." Rather than get into an argument about it, I realized that I needed to show him how many steps there were and how long each step would take. Intuitively, I chose to begin with his turning in the report and working backwards through the steps.

When he had the whole picture of the process in front of him, I then asked, "So, Josh, when do you need to start?" Without taking his eyes off the picture he replied, "Right now." End of discussion. No argument. He now had a concrete picture of the project and how much time it was going to take.

Proving once again that there is no such thing as a new idea, I'd been teaching Planning Ahead by Planning Backwards for years, thinking it was my own invention. No. Some professionals may recognize the process by the term back-chaining. (As a visual thinker, the term back-chaining gives me a really odd, confusing mental picture, so I never use it!)

The following process, which uses separate sticky notes for each step of a project, can be used in many situations beyond planning time for academic assignments. Adult clients have used it for planning engineering projects and grant writing. A friend who is an architect uses it to plan projects, and I used it to publish this book.

For the purposes of this course, I use an example of a high school research paper. Projects that require writing are good to use because students often have incomplete pictures of the steps needed to produce quality work. You may adjust the example to fit your client. If they have a specific project due, or something else they want to plan, go with that.

MATERIALS NEEDED:

- Dry erase board, markers, and eraser
- For each participant (parents included) a copy of the *Seeing*

Key Points

1. To meet deadlines, plan backwards from the point of completion.

2. Use sticky notes with simple drawings for each step and include a short word label.

3. Assign time estimates to each step, using filled-in circles to represent the space of time required for each step.

Tip

Students often don't understand the value of the effort put into extra credit. If I am working with students, I explain that a typical middle school teacher might be grading fifty to a hundred reports on pyramids. They slog through them, checking off a list to see if you remembered to include everything. If you did include all the requirements *and* also took the time to write a paragraph that talks about the importance of cats to ancient Egyptians (because you found it interesting), then that wakes up that teacher. She thinks, "Wow! Something different! Extra credit points!" Those points can make the difference between an A and a B, or between a B and a C.

My Time workbook
- Sharp pencils with erasers
- 2″ x 1 1/2″ sticky notes, twelve for each participant

WHAT I DO:

1. **Direct** participants to page 31. Pass out sticky notes to all participants.

2. **Explain** to the participants that by using sticky notes, they are going to break a project down into steps and estimate how long each step is going to take. After drawing the project expectations, this is the next stage of getting a project done on time.

3. **Describe** the imaginary project as a history research paper, seven pages long, which will be worth 40 percent of the class grade.

4. On the dry erase board, **draw** a box in the lower right corner and **explain** that it represents a sticky note.

5. **Draw** the following, **explaining** as you draw:

   - Two stick figures in the box. One is the student. One is the teacher

   - Both have smiles on their faces.

   - The student has a paper in her hand.

   - They are smiling because quality work is being turned in on time. Example:

ACTIVITY:

1. **Direct** participants to take one sticky note and put it over the box in the lower right corner of page 31, which has a star in it. Have them copy the figures you drew on the dry erase board.

2. Once they are done drawing, **direct** them to place a second sticky note over the box to the left of the first one.

3. **Ask:** What was the last thing you had to do with that paper in order to be able to turn it in to the teacher?

   • Wrong answers: Write it, print it off, staple it, etc. (If they guess wrong and get stuck, I tantalize them by telling them that if I had a nickel for every time a student forgets to do this step I'd have a lot of money.)

   • Correct answer: Put it in my backpack/bag so it gets to school. (Remembering to put finished work in their back-pack is a common issue for students with executive func-tioning challenges. I include drawing this step to give them a mental picture of themselves putting it into the backpack.)

4. **Direct** participants to draw a picture of them putting the paper (in a binder) into a backpack.

5. **Ask:** How long does it take to get that paper into the backpack?

   • Wrong answers: Thirty seconds or one minute

   • Correct answer: It depends upon how long it takes you to get your backpack. If it is downstairs and you have go get it and get distracted along the way, it takes more than a minute!

6. **Explain** that they should allow five minutes for this step. If it takes less—no problem. Have them draw a clock circle on the sticky note and fill in a sliver of the circle to represent five minutes. Example:

7. **Proceed** to have participants draw sticky notes for each of the following twelve steps, always answering the question: What were you doing just before this last step?

- Be sure to **add** the time-estimate circles to each sticky note.

- Always **tell** students/writers to pad their time estimates. Writing takes longer than they think it will.

- **Recommend** allowing an hour per page for each of the steps: from first draft to second revision to final revision and editing. If they don't end up using all that planned time, that's great. They'll have free time for fun.

Twelve Steps for Writing a Paper:

*Planning from End to Beginning**

*Time estimates are based on a seven-page paper

Step 1: Turning it in on time

Step 2: Putting it in backpack (5 minutes)

Step 3: Final printing, doing a last check for errors, stapling, or placing in a report cover (15 minutes)

Step 4: Final revision and editing corrections (1 hour per page—7 hours, depending on number of corrections per page)

Step 5: Final editor review (15–30 minutes)

Tip for Step 5:

Students tend to leave out the final editing process of having another set of eyes look for errors or ask final questions about clarity. Final editors can be parents, siblings, friends in college, or peers with good writing skills. If students struggle with writing, they may require an additional editing step with a teacher or writing tutor.

Step 6: First revision (7+ hours, depending on the quality of the first draft)

Step 7: Editing by an editor (30–60 minutes of conference time)

Tip for Step 7:

The first edit requires an editor other than the writer. This editing is for the following:

1. Ideas and content
2. Organization and flow
3. Clarity
4. Word choice
5. Voice
6. Conventions: spelling, punctuation, and grammar

Step 8: First draft (7+ hours, depending on writing skills)

Step 9: Outlining (30–60 minutes)

Tip #1 for Step 9:

Students often leave out the critical step of outlining or planning their writing. They just sit down and start writing, putting in time and effort that often requires significant changes once an editor goes over it. This is very discouraging for the writer.

Have participants put a star sticker (or a drawn star) on this sticky note, stressing that if they do this step, the rest of the writing process will flow more easily and take a lot less time.

Tip #2 for Step 9:

Alternatives to traditional outlines work best for many visually oriented minds. They can use graphic organizers, mind maps, or sticky notes to get the initial picture of how the paper will be organized. After this step, they can create a traditional outline.

Step 10: Research, reading, and note taking (7 hours, depending on the project and the student's reading abilities)

Step 11: Gathering resources (2+ hours)

Tip for Step 11:

Students may need to make a trip to a library. Don't forget to include travel time and time spent looking for books in the stacks and in the on-line card catalog, as well as looking for resources on the Internet.

Step 12: Drawing My Assignment: line by line, drawing out the expectations for the project (30+ minutes)

Tip for Step 12:

Stress that drawing the directions to the assignment is another *critical* step that deserves a sticky star. This should be done on the same day that the assignment is received.

Remind them to write due dates on their calendar.

9. **Direct** participants to add up the time circles to see how much total time is required to turn in a quality written project. Have them write the total number of hours required across the top of page 31.

10. **Direct:** Have them put foil stars on the sticky notes for outlining and Drawing My Assignment. If these two steps are done, then the whole writing process will go much more easily. (If you don't get foil stars, have them just draw stars on those sticky notes.)

11. **Discuss** their thoughts about writing a paper after doing this process. What have they learned? What steps would they have left out? Could this be a useful set of strategies for them to use in the future to get things done on deadline?

Page 32:
Planning the Time to Do the Steps

Planning the Time to Do the Steps

The next step required to finish projects on time is to schedule the time to do the steps. This is where you need to use a Month Calendar because it will give a view of the future space available to work on the project.

MATERIALS NEEDED:

- Sticky notes completed for activity on page 31
- For each participant (parents included) a copy of the *Seeing My Time* workbook
- Sharp pencils with erasers

WHAT I DO:

1. **Direct** participants to remove all the sticky notes from the activity on page 31, one by one, in order, and place them on the table in front of them. (NOTE: This will make it possible for participants to easily place the sticky notes onto page 32.)

2. **Direct** participants to the undated sample calendar on page 32. (NOTE: If your client is planning for a real project rather than the imaginary student paper, do this next step on a current Month Calendar.)

3. **Say:** Projects have to fit around the rest of our lives: work, homework, and scheduled activities like sports, family events, and parties. We are going to use our sticky note steps to plan backwards to find the time to do the project.

4. **Explain** that first they are going to create imaginary commitments for this imaginary month. Have them block out some weekend afternoons for things that might really take up their time—soccer games, out-of-town guests, etc. Put down other possible commitments during the week—meetings or events in the evenings. Students might put down exams that will require studying. Example:

Key Points

1. Projects have to fit around homework.

2. Projects have to fit around the scheduled activities of everyday life.

3. Use a Month Calendar and sticky notes to find the space and time to do projects.

4. Plan to finish a project **two days** before the deadline.

	Wednesday	Thursday	Friday	Saturday
3	4	5	6	7 *Soccer game*
			H.S. Football game	
10 *math test*	11	12	13	14
		school Play		*Tom's BD Party*
17	18	19	20	21

ACTIVITY:

1. **Direct** participants to write the words *paper due* on the 31st of the month.

2. **Direct** participants to place the sticky note that shows turning in the work on time over the box for the 31st.

3. **Direct** participants to write the words *paper done* on the 29th of the month.

4. **Ask:** Why should you have the paper done two days before it is due?

5. **Answer:** Life happens.

   • The power goes out so you can't use your printer.
   • The printer runs out of ink.
   • You run out of paper.
   • Your computer decides to die.

6. **Say:** These extra two days give you a cushion for disasters to happen and still get your project done on time.

7. **Direct** participants to place the next sticky note, the one putting the project in the backpack, over the words *paper done* on the 29th.

8. **Explain** that they will now decide when to do the remaining steps, placing the sticky notes over those dates.

- Some days may have room for a couple of steps to get completed, so it is OK to put more than one sticky note on a given day.

- The final sticky note should be placed over Monday the 2nd, as this is the imaginary day the project was assigned.

9. **Ask** participants if they have any questions about how to use sticky notes and a calendar to plan the time to get projects done. Can they imagine a project that might require using such a strategy?

Page 33:
Getting It Done
and Reaching Goals

This page gives the participants time to pause and review in their minds the strategies and steps required to get projects done on time. These include:

- Drawing My Assignment—make sure that you understand the expectations for the project by drawing and using a highlighter

- Breaking a project into steps by using sticky notes and planning backwards

- Estimating time needed for each step by drawing time circles

- Using a Month Calendar and the sticky notes to find the time to work on the steps

ACTIVITY:

1. **Direct** participants to turn to page 33 and have them write the steps needed to get a project done on time.

2. **Discuss** their answers and have them fill in any of the key steps they may have left out. Possible answers:

   - Draw the assignment or directions.

   - Use sticky notes to break it into steps.

   - Estimate the time needed for each step.

   - Find the space and time to work on the project by planning backwards from the date of completion.

   - Use a Month Calendar with sticky notes.

Page 34:
To Get It Done—Just Start

Getting started—task initiation—is often a problem for people with executive functioning challenges. But once they start a project, many find it is easy to keep working on it.

WHAT I DO:

1. **Direct** participants to page 34.

2. **Say:** Getting started on a project can be hard for lots of reasons. However, once you start a project, it is often easy to keep working on it. Committing to starting a project and putting it into your week's planning will get a project done.

ACTIVITY:

1. **Direct** participants to draw or write answers to the two questions in the box on page 34.

2. **Share** responses.

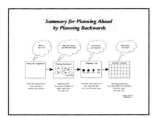

Page 35:
Summary for Planning Ahead
by Planning Backwards

This page is used as a visual reminder of the steps used in the process of Planning Ahead by Planning Backwards.

Breaking a complex project into concrete visual steps is necessary to compensate for executive skill deficits in planning, prioritizing, and time management. Estimating time and using the visual cue of time circles helps to keep the space of time required to complete the work in the mind of the time-challenged.

WHAT I DO:

1. **Direct** participants to page 35.

2. **Explain** that it is a visual summary of the steps they just went through as they planned ahead by planning backwards. It shows how to break a project into steps and find the time to do it.

3. **Explain** that this page is for reference to use when they get their next project to plan.

Unit 5: Organization and Paper Management

Key Points

1. All things need a home—someplace where you can find them.

2. Disorganized papers and belongings cause stress.

3. Binders are portable filing cabinets.

4. During a rushed day, have just one folder or inbox in which to put all papers so they don't get lost.

5. Set aside one time, each day, to organize the paper in your inbox.

6. People lose papers, including teachers. Protect yourself.

7. Planners are your best friend for keeping track of assignments, but have a back-up plan.

Tip

If organizing a binder is a big issue for a student, you might plan to set aside session time to create the binder; otherwise it is expected that the binder will be created as a homework assignment.

Organization is an executive functioning skill that indirectly affects time management and getting things done. The time-challenged can spend a lot of time looking for missing or lost important papers. They also struggle with keeping track of objects in their lives, like cell phones and keys. They can have binders, backpacks, desks, and rooms overflowing with piles.

This unit will provide opportunities to consider personal solutions for handling the possessions and papers that fill their lives. Strategies will be built upon the First Truth of Time: Out of Sight, Out of Mind. Please note that managing possessions is only given two pages of brief discussion in this course. If your clients have major organization issues with possessions (a home in a state of chaos), they might require the help of a professional organizer, as those needs are beyond the scope of this program.

The discussion on handling papers and creating a useful binder/planner requires using specific products that I have found essential. Since some of the recommended items can be difficult to locate at an office supply store, I have made items available under Cool Tools on my website, www.ExecutiveFunctioningSuccess.com. I provide this service to support my clients in easily getting the items they need.

This unit also includes a few pages dedicated to exploring issues beyond organization that affect the success experienced by the time-challenged at school and work.

Topics in this unit include:

- Where to keep key objects that are often misplaced

- How to start cleaning up piles
- Handling papers at school, work, and home
- Designing and using a personal planner in a binder
- Having a backup system for lost information
- Being prepared for classes or meetings
- Multitasking and focus

Covering all the material in this unit may not be possible in a single session. Complete any unfinished pages at the beginning of the next session.

MATERIALS NEEDED:

- Dry erase board, markers, and eraser
- For each participant (parents included) a copy of the *Seeing My Time* workbook
- Sharp pencils with erasers
- 3 x 5 cards

A sample binder to show how to organize a binder. It should contain the following:

- A two-pocket transparent plastic folder to use as an inbox and an outbox
- Two-pocket insertable plastic pocket dividers
- Easy-access sheet protectors
- Month Calendar with a two-page view for each month

Key Points

1. Being able to organize is an executive function of the brain.

2. To help a brain that can't organize, assign items a home, or specific location, where they belong and where you can find them in a hurry.

Page 37:
Organization
and Paper Management

The time-challenged often struggle with keeping track of the possessions in their lives. Deficits in working memory and sustained focus make it easy to forget where things like keys and cell phones were last set down. They easily go out of sight and out of mind.

The solution is to spend some time developing metacognitive awareness of why this issue exists and to plan to assign "home" locations for the storage of these often misplaced objects.

WHAT I DO:

1. **Direct** participants to page 37.

2. **Explain** that the ability to keep track of our stuff is the executive functioning skill of organization that was talked about during the first hour together. Some brains are better at it than others.

3. **Explain** that being disorganized can be very stressful:

   • Expensive belongings like cell phones and iPods are lost or misplaced.

   • Keys can't be found when you need to leave the house.

   • Important papers are hard to find when you need them.

4. **Explain** that the key to helping a brain that struggles with organization is to follow the words on page 37: *Things need a home.* Everything needs a single, predictable place where you can find it.

Story About Keys

I once had five sets of keys because I could never remember which pocket, purse, shelf, or dresser I'd put them on. I spent a lot of frantic time looking for keys, which contributed to my being late a lot.

Electronic car keys are too expensive for multiple sets, so now my keys go back to their home in the back pocket of my purse. My purse goes to its home on a chair in the dining room. This works for me ninety-nine per cent of the time. The other one percent of the time? I'm frantically running around looking for my purse.

ACTIVITY:

1. **Direct** participants to answer the prompt on page 37: *What things do I keep misplacing?*

2. **Share** responses and problem solve where a good home for each item might be located.

Key Points

1. Being disorganized adds to stress.

2. Tackle organizing using the mantra *little by little*.

3. Use timers to motivate you to clean and organize.

Page 38:
" . . . but I can't find it."

Out-of-control piles plague the time-challenged. Clean clothes are buried under dirty clothes. Important documents are buried in piles of paper. The house is so messy that it is embarrassing to have company over.

The clutter in the living environment spills into the brain, causing stress. The disorganized get distracted by the desire to clean up and create order, and then get bogged down when they try to clean it all up at once. It is easy to be overwhelmed by the mess, which makes it hard to get anything done.

This page suggests a strategy of using a timer to begin the process of de-cluttering and organizing personal spaces.

WHAT I DO:

1. **Direct** participants to page 38.

2. **Explain** that the time-challenged tend to use an organization system called "the pile." The value of the pile is that it creates the illusion that we won't lose something if we can somehow keep it in sight. This can work for a couple of little piles, but piles quickly get out of control.

3. **Explain** that it is very easy for out-of-control piles in the living environment to add stress to the brain because we end up unable to find what we need when we need it.

4. **Explain** that when the stress becomes too much, the decision is made to clean up and get organized. This is fine, but it is impossible to get organized all at one time. There aren't enough hours in the day. (Think back to those empty spaces in your week.)

   The time-challenged start cleaning with the best of intentions, and then get bogged down or neglect other pressing needs, which ultimately adds more stress.

5. **Explain** that a realistic plan for organizing is following the mantra *little by little* . . .

ACTIVITY:

1. **Direct** participants to write on page 38 where they have piles and to share their responses.

2. **Explain** the following strategy for getting organized:

   • Plan five- to fifteen-minute cleaning sprees into your day.

   • Pick one spot—a drawer, a corner, a dresser top—that needs organizing.

   • Set a timer for the amount of time you have to clean and go!

   • Stop when the timer goes off so you don't neglect other things you need to do.

3. **Explain** that they'll be amazed at how much clearing out they can do in a week of little bits of time—little by little they will indeed get their belongings organized and do away with the teetering piles.

   This is where I often suggest that they start a charity bag in a closet. As they organize, they should be looking for items that they no longer use or want. Putting them in the charity bag is the next step to organizing—getting rid of excess stuff.

A Story About Cleaning

I have had great success motivating myself to clean using a timer. Once, a greasy teakettle was bugging me, but I didn't feel like I had the time to scour it. One day, I set a timer for five minutes, promising myself that I'd quit when it went off, even if I wasn't done with the kettle. I was amazed: I was done in four minutes and twenty-nine seconds!

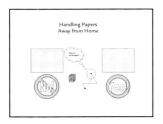

Key Points

1. When you don't have time to file, temporarily put all papers into just one folder or inbox.

2. Clean out your inbox daily.

Page 39: Handling Papers Away from Home

Students especially are guilty of stuffing papers out of sight into random places. They may have a vague memory of putting that important paper somewhere but can't remember where they might have put it. The solutions is to have one easily accessible place to put all incoming papers.

For students the most successful solution I've found is to have one plastic transparent folder that is used as the inbox or home for all pieces of paper collected during the school day. Ideally the folder should have holes punched in it so it can fit in a three-ring binder. Adults can have a pocket in their planner.

Dramatizing the Challenge of Organizing Papers at School

When I work with students, I do a little role-playing scene to emphasize the problem of organizing papers at school. I play the rushed teacher who, just as the end-of-class bell rings, says, "Wait! Wait! Take these papers home. This one needs to be signed by your parents. This one is a graded assignment. This one explains the project we are starting tomorrow—don't lose it. And this one is your math homework. OK. Hurry! You'll be late for the bus!"

I ask the students if this has ever happened to them. They always nod yes. I ask what they do with the papers. "Stuff them in my backpack" is the typical answer. And we all know that backpacks are really just mini black holes.

WHAT I DO:

1. **Direct** participants to page 39.

2. **Explain:** During busy school or work days, people are often handed papers and don't have time to file them where they will be able to find them later. The temptation is to stuff them somewhere with the plan of getting back to them. This sets up the situation of forgetting or misplacing important papers because they're out of sight and out of mind.

ACTIVITY:

1. **Direct** participants to the box above the word *No!* on page 39.

2. **Ask** participants to write or draw places they should not stuff papers—places where papers get lost and forgotten. Possible answers might include the following:

   - Backpacks or bags
   - Folded into books
   - Lockers
   - Pockets
   - Randomly stuffed into a binder or briefcase

3. **Ask** participants to share where they shouldn't put papers.

4. **Say:** To solve this paper-management problem, you need to set up a temporary home for all incoming papers.

5. **Show** them an example of a durable transparent plastic two-pocket folder that has been punched for a three-ring binder. The transparency is important because you can see the contents, which helps to keep the papers in mind. Plastic folders are very durable—unlike their paper counterparts.

   (I buy these in bulk and give one to each student because I feel it is critical for them to have this folder to use immediately. It can be difficult to find a transparent pocket folder, so I offer choices under Cool Tools on my website: www.ExecutiveFunctioningSuccess.com.)

6. **Explain** that adults will need either a durable folder or binder pocket in their planner.

7. **Direct** participants to the box above the word *Yes!* on page 39. Have them draw a pocket folder as the correct place to put incoming papers when they are away from home.

Tip

I warn students against putting folded important papers into text books. I joke that books must be magical like in *Harry Potter* because we've almost all left a folded piece of paper in a book and then been unable to find it when we needed it. And then—a day or two later—there it is, right where you put it!

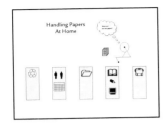

Key Points

1. It takes less than five minutes to go through your inbox if you do it every day.

2. Empty your inbox *every day*.

3. Your inbox must not become a pile in a folder.

Page 40:
Handling Papers at Home

Emptying the inbox daily is the critical next step to paper management. While I often tell clients to pad the time it takes to do something, it really does take less than five minutes to go through an inbox if you do it daily.

What confounds many people with organizational challenges is what to do with each piece of paper. The activity on this page sets up the metacognition needed by providing a sequence of actions to consider for each piece of paper. These actions are:

- Recycle it.
- Give it to someone else who needs to see it.
- Write a date on a calendar.
- File it.
- Do it and put it in the proper place in your binder—the plastic folder that becomes the outbox for papers that need to return to school or work.
- Put it (in your binder or folder) back in your backpack/bag/briefcase to get it back to school or work.

WHAT I DO:

1. **Direct** participants to page 40.

2. **Explain** that when students first sit down to begin homework, or adults first sit down at their desk, it is time to empty the inbox. The following activity will show them what to do with each piece of paper.

ACTIVITY:

1. **Explain** that going through the inbox daily really does take less than five minutes.

2. **Direct** participants to the first box on the left on page 40—the one with the recycle symbol.

   - **Explain** that some of the papers you collect during a day just don't have any value. You are done with them. So get rid of them.

   - **Direct** participants to write the word *recycle* in the box with the recycling symbol.

3. **Explain** that some papers need to be passed off to someone else, like a parent or spouse, for them to see and deal with. Or perhaps the piece of paper has an important date on it for an event that you don't want to miss. Immediately put that date on your Month Calendar.

4. **Direct** participants to write the words *for others* and *put on calendar* in the second box.

5. **Explain** that some papers need to be kept where you can easily find them later. For students this might be a page that they will need to work on later in class.

6. **Direct** participants to write the word *file* in the middle box.

   • Students would be filing into their binder pockets.

   • Adults would be filing into permanent file folders or a tickler file that will remind them to deal with the paper later.

7. **Explain** that the fourth box is for papers that need immediate action.

   • For students this would be something like homework for tonight.

   • For adults it might represent a bill to be paid or a phone call that can be done in less than three minutes.

8. **Direct** participants to write the words *do it* in the fourth box.

9. **Explain** that when you are done with a piece of paper and it is ready to go back to someone else—a teacher or coworker— you need to put it in the outbox.

   • **Explain** that the outbox is actually the front pocket of your inbox folder. If you put a paper facing up in the front of the folder you will be able to see it and be reminded to turn it over to the teacher or coworker.

   • **Direct** participants to write the words: *backpack*, *bag*, and *outbox* on the final box of the page.

10. **Explain** that at home they will make a pile for each of these

boxes. If they choose, they can even make sticky note labels for each pile to help remember the steps.

Using a Tickler File

This brief description of a tickler file is from my blog at my website:

THE TICKLER FILE

I'd never heard of a tickler file until my son introduced me to *Getting Things Done* by David Allen. Apparently the idea has been around a long time. But for me, the tickler file was a revelation and a godsend. I recommend tickler files to my ADHD and time-challenged clients with executive functioning issues.

WHAT IS A TICKLER FILE?

The tickler file is a holding zone for pieces of paper that need to surface back into your consciousness at a future point in time. It's a kind of reminder system. For instance, if a flyer comes in the mail for a course that sounds interesting, but you're not ready to sign up, you put it in the tickler file. If the registration date is in six weeks, you've got time to think about it. You look quickly ahead to date when you will have to decide and register—say on the 12th of the month. You pop the flyer into the folder labeled 12. You don't need to think about it again until the 12th of the month when you open the file. I also use mine for reminder notes and things like tickets and birthday cards.

TICKLER FILE BASICS:

In its simplest form, a tickler file is composed of two sets of file folders. One set is numbered 1–31 so you have a folder dedicated to each day of a month. The other set has one folder for each month of the year. I made mine using reinforced file folders that stay looking nice longer than standard file folders. Then I used a label maker for the wording and numbers. The label maker creates a professional look, and looks are important. You want to be motivated to use this file!

HOW TO USE IT:

The numbered files go in front with the months in order behind them. If today is the 6th, then that file should be on top. Each day open the file for the day and either handle the paper or delay it by putting it in a file for a future date. When you are done with the file for the 6th, put it back in your tickler file, behind the next month and the file for the 5th.

Try making a tickler file. It's made a real difference in my paper management.

Page 41:
Creating a Useful Binder

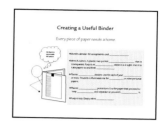

A properly designed binder is a very useful tool for the time-challenged. My binder/planner supports my whole life. Unfortunately, most prepackaged binders come with unnecessary pages and dividers that get in the way of organizing for the time-challenged—too many options and choices and forms.

The guiding principles for binders or planners is to keep them simple and to follow the rules: 1) Out of Sight, Out of Mind and 2) Things Need a Home. I encourage clients to design the interior of their binders to meet their needs.

The binder itself needs to be sturdy, not too bulky, and easily accessible. Middle school students show up with heavy binders that have all sorts of bells and whistles that are marketed specifically to this age group. They are full of pockets where papers are stuffed and lost because they are out of sight. These binders often fall apart before the year is half over. I suggest sturdy plastic binders as a lightweight alternative. The options vary from store to store.

For adults I encourage clients to search around for a binder they really like, that feels good to touch and is aesthetically pleasing. Visual and tactile learners are more likely to use a tool if it is attractive to them.

MATERIALS NEEDED:

A sample binder to show how to organize a binder. It should contain the following:

- A two-pocket transparent plastic folder to use as an inbox and an outbox
- Two-pocket insertable plastic pocket dividers

I recommend plastic pocket dividers for two reasons: they are sturdier than paper versions and most of the time-challenged would rather put papers quickly into a pocket versus taking the time to punch them with three holes, open up the binder, and put them in.

Remember, we want to keep it simple and easy.

- Easy-access sheet protectors

Key Points

1. A binder is a portable filing cabinet.

2. A binder should have a folder dedicated to being the inbox and outbox.

3. A two-page spread month calendar works well for recording assignments and appointments.

Tip

Products come and go in the office-supply world. I get attached to using one, and they discontinue it. On my website, under Cool Tools, I'll have the most appropriate transparent two-pocket folder I can find. It might require punching holes in it to put it in the front of a binder.

• A two-page Month Calendar

I recommend that students use this calendar for recording their assignments because it gives a better picture of the future and is less bulky than the planners provided by schools. Since it is in the binder, it doesn't get lost like the smaller, separate planners often do.

However you do it, it is important to have visual examples of the materials so parents can make a shopping list, or you can direct them to my website: www.ExecutiveFunctioningSuccess. com, where under Cool Tools they will find links to appropriate binder items.

WHAT I DO:

1. **Direct** participants to page 41.

2. **Explain** that this page shows participants how to create a really useful binder that will support their organizational needs. Stress these points:

   • A good binder is really just a portable filing cabinet.

   • Every piece of paper in it should be in its home so that you can find it quickly when you need it.

   • It is also a place to keep your Month Calendar to be used for writing down assignments and appointments.

   • It should not become a holder for a pile of paper. It needs to be periodically cleaned out so outdated, filed papers are recycled.

ACTIVITY:

Direct participants to the box on page 41. As you read the sentences, have them fill in the blanks with the correct answer, which is shown in bold print here.

   • Month Calendar: for assignments and **appointments**

   • Inbox and outbox: A plastic two-pocket **folder** that is transparent. Keep it on **top** where it is in sight. Use it to take papers to and from **school** or **work**.

Tip

As part of the cost of the course, I provide students with the plastic pocket folder for the inbox, a set of five plastic pocket dividers, and a couple of easy-access sheet protectors to help them organize a binder. I do this because parents are often too busy or they forget to go shopping for the necessary pieces. This way I can start the binder reorganization process before the students go home.

- Plastic **pocket** dividers: one for each of your **subjects** or roles. Students often need one for their **doodles** or other personal papers.

  If they don't have a home pocket for doodles, drawings, poetry, etc., those papers will sabotage a paper management system.

- Plastic **sheet** protectors: Use for paper that you need to keep **safe** and separate so you don't **lose** it.

  It is a good idea to put directions for projects in sheet protectors. Then they are placed behind the subject pocket divider so they can be found quickly and easily.

- Keep it tidy: Empty inbox **daily**.

ACTIVITY:

This is an **optional** activity depending on the time you have in your session. I always ask students to bring their backpack/bag to this session along with their binder. I try to take time to at least sort through the collected pile—recycling what is old before helping them to file the remaining papers into the appropriate pocket divider. Labeling all the dividers may have to be done on their own. Just be sure that you give them enough of a picture of what to do to complete the project at home.

The Planner: Your Best Friend—
Use It

Key Points

1. A planner needs to be easy to use.

2. It needs to stay with you throughout the day.

3. Assignments need to be written down in two places: the date you get it *and* the date it is due.

4. You need a backup system for your schedule.

Tip

While many adults want a smaller organizer, I find that the little paper size is awkward because many of the papers in my life are 8 1/2″ by 11″, so the small organizers don't make a good portable filing cabinet. That's why I use a full-sized binder. And I can easily make my own forms for that larger format.

Page 42:
The Planner:
Your Best Friend—Use It

Students and adults with executive functioning challenges need to use planners for time management. The planner is support for weak working memory and keeps a to-do list in sight, as well as being critical for weekly planning needed to reach long-term goals.

Today many people use a variety of electronic devices as their planners. These can be very useful. I confess to preferring a paper-based binder since it just seems easier and quicker to use. A two-page Month Calendar gives me a much bigger picture of my time than a small view on a phone screen. It comes down to personal preference. The guiding principal is to keep it simple and easy to use so that it actually gets used!

My Thoughts on Student Planners

Many schools require students to purchase and use a specific planner or assignment book.

Most of these planners have two problems. First, they are often small and get lost. Second, they focus on giving students a view of only a week at a time. Turn the page, and those assignments are . . . out of sight, out of mind. They don't get a picture of either the past or the future.

For these reasons, I recommend using a simple binder-sized, two-page month calendar that is kept in the front of the student's primary binder. You can get them in office supply stores.

If you have a good alternative for using the school planner, many teachers are flexible.

WHAT I DO:

1.   **Direct** participants to page 42.

2.   **Say:** In our busy lives, we move around a lot and need a quick and easy way to record information that needs to be handled or put onto our calendar. It is dangerous and often unrealistic to count on our working memory to help us remember to do things.

3. **Say:** Students and adults both need planners or organizers. Different planners fit different situations. It can take some experimenting to find what works for you. The important thing is to have a way to capture what you need to do. Whatever you choose—it needs to be simple and easy, and hard to lose. Look at office supply stores and online for options.

4. **Discuss** some options to consider for a good planner:

    • Carry an organizer binder like those made by Day Timer or Franklin Covey.

    • Create your own as described in the last activity on page 42.

    • Use a small pocket monthly calendar.

    • Use the calendar function on your phone.

ACTIVITY:

1. **Direct** participants to turn to page 42 and answer the first prompt: *What makes a good planner?*

    Answers:
    • Simple
    • Easy to use
    • Hard to lose

2. **Direct** participants to answer the second prompt: *Where should I keep it?*

    Answers:
    • With me all the time
    • Within easy reach
    • In sight

3. **Say:** When we are given something to do that has a due date in the distant future, it is important to write it down in two places: on the day you get the assignment *and* on the actual due date.

    By writing it down in these two places, we are focusing our attention on the task, which will help us to put the task into our long-term memory. It also keeps the task in sight in more than one place, and thus in mind more often.

4. **Direct** participants to answer the third prompt: *Where should I write assignments that are due in the future?*

    Answer: On the day it is assigned and on the day it is due.

5. **Say:** Sometimes we drop the ball and don't have our planner with us. We need a backup system to record information or a plan to retrieve it from another source. **Suggest** these options to consider:

    • Carry a very small notepad in your pocket or bag and daily transfer notes onto your calendar or week plan.

    • Use a sturdy binder clip and attach a 3 x 5 card to your notebook or wallet. Transfer notes from the card to your calendar for planning.

    • Use electronic devices like your phone to send yourself messages or notes about what you need to put on your calendar.

    • And, yes, while it is not my first choice, you can write it on your hand in ink.

    • Get help! Students should have a couple of backup buddies in each class and get their contact numbers.

    I encourage students to figure out at least two people in each of their classes who are the kind of person who will have the assignment information that my clients might forget or lose.

    Likewise, I encourage parents to make contacts with other parents so they can get information regarding what their child may be confused about.

6. **Direct** participants to answer the fourth prompt: *Other ways to keep my assignments or reminders.*

    Answers:
    • Small notepads
    • 3 x 5 cards
    • Send yourself a message
    • Call a friend

Page 43:
Papers Get Lost
and Computers Die

Key Point
Have a backup plan in case papers are lost or a computer dies.

Missing papers are a major stressor for the individual with an organizational deficit. It is very easy for important papers to get misplaced or lost. It is crucial for individuals to have a backup plan.

This is especially important for students who have a history of not turning in work. I assure my students that some teachers are prone to losing papers because they may get hundreds in a day, and they may have organizational issues too. I tell them that if a teacher loses a paper, it is the student who will be blamed every time. It's not fair; it's just the way it is when you have a history of late or missing work.

Everyone should have a computer backup plan. Computers have a way of dying at the worst possible time, making it impossible to access some important paper or project on the hard drive.

WHAT I DO:

1. **Direct** participants to page 43.

2. **Explain:** There are several ways to make backup plans for important papers. Options include:

   • Computer files can go on an external thumb drive.

   • Email completed papers to teachers or professors. This leaves a trail of proof.

   • Back up your computer's hard drive onto a server or external hard drive.

   • Photocopy or scan papers that are not done on the computer.

   • Take pictures of projects and email them to teachers.

ACTIVITY:

1. **Direct** participants to turn to page 43 and write the options for backup plans to avoid losing important information.

2. **Discuss** their answers and have them fill in any of options they may have forgotten. Share responses.

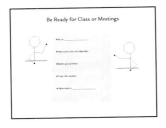

Key Point

To be ready for a class or a meeting, you have to prepare—organize—your mind as well as your materials.

Page 44:
Be Ready for Class or Meetings

Master teacher Tim McGee produced a DVD titled *How to Become a SuperStar Student*. In it, he stresses the importance of being prepared for class, and that doesn't mean just having pencils and paper. He means having your mind ready to learn.

The purpose of this page is to get the disorganized mind to think about why it needs to be ready for class and how to be ready to be a successful learner.

WHAT I DO:

1. **Direct** participants to page 44.

2. **Say:** In order to be ready to learn and participate in class or meetings, we have to be prepared, organized. It is not only our materials that need to be prepared—it is our mind as well.

ACTIVITY:

1. **Say:** If we show up late to a class or a meeting, we are stressed and not in an optimal state of mind for learning. Being on time is the first step in being ready for class or meetings.

2. **Read** the first line in the box on page 44. Direct participants to fill in the first line with the word *time*.

    Ask which Time Tools they can use to ensure they get to class or meetings on time.

    Direct them to write their choices below the first line.

    Answers:
    - Timers
    - Cell phone alarms
    - Alarm clocks
    - Watch alarms

3. **Say:** Likewise, if we show up without necessary materials— our assignments, meeting agendas, a pencil and paper for notes—our brain is going to be distracted from learning and paying attention.

4. **Direct** participants to the second line and have them write or draw the materials they need to bring to class or meetings.

5. **Remind** participants about the first session and the discussion about how learning is connecting new information to old information in the brain.

    Explain that warming up your brain for a class or a meeting means putting in a little review time to cover material that is going to be discussed.

    By going over notes, looking ahead at the material that is going to be covered, or going over meeting agendas, your brain is getting ready to maximize its learning. You know what is coming, so you can connect old knowledge with the new material that will be presented in the class or meeting. You will spend less time in confusion and will be able to focus better on the new material.

6. **Direct** participants to the third line and have them write or draw what they need to do to warm up their brain.

7. **Remind** participants about the First Rule of Time: Out of Sight, Out of Mind. Tracking the teacher or speaker means that you should keep your eyes on the speaker.

    If visual thinkers look away at something else, they tend to miss what the speaker says. I tell students to imagine a laser beam that connects their eyes to their teacher's eyes. As the teacher moves around the room speaking, follow her with your eyes.

8. **Direct** participants to the fourth line and have them write or draw what it means to track the teacher.

9. **Say:** In order to be on time, to have your necessary tools and materials, and to warm up your brain, you have to plan the space and time to prepare for your class or meeting.

10. **Direct** participants to the last line and have them fill in the blank with the word *prepare*.

Page 45:
The Brain Is *Not* Designed for Multitasking

There is a pervasive myth in our culture that by multitasking, we are using our time and our brain more efficiently. Wrong. John Medina, molecular biologist and author of *Brain Rules: 12 Principles for Surviving and Thriving at Work, Home and School*, dispels this myth. It turns out that the brain can only do one thing at a time, and the more we demand it to quickly shift between tasks, the slower we are and the more errors we make. Folks who seem to pull off multitasking well actually have above average working memory.

Time-challenged and ADHD adults and adolescents don't like hearing that they aren't good at multitasking. They will claim to be masters of it. Today, sitting at a computer screen is an open door to multitasking opportunities and demands: multiple screens open, email, live chat, instant messaging, Facebook, and YouTube videos all vie for attention. All this multitasking could explain why homework takes so long to do!

WHAT I DO:

1. **Direct** participants to page 45.

2. **Explain** that multitasking to get more done is a myth. The brain can only do one thing at a time. When we ask it to multitask—change quickly back and forth between different tasks—we actually work more slowly and make more errors. So to work efficiently, we need to focus our brain on one task at a time. To do this, we have to limit the distractions in our work environment.

ACTIVITY:

1. **Discuss** the typical distractions or multitasking activities that each participant experiences.

2. **Say:** Now that you understand that distractions have a negative effect on you productivity, write in the box on page 45 what would be the optimal work environment for you.

    (Working with music playing while doing homework is often an issue between parents and students. The Journal of Child

Psychology and Psychiatry reported that for ADHD students, some noise or music benefits performance, but that it deteriorates performance in normal students. Personally, if I have music playing it needs to be instrumental only or vocals in another language. Otherwise I get distracted by the visuals in my mind produced by the words in the song.)

Unit 6:
The Third Truth of Time

The Way You Use Your Time Equals Your Life

Key Points

1. Use the strategy of Planning Ahead by Planning Backwards to reach future dreams and goals.

2. Be realistic about the time needed to change time-management behavior.

The very nature of the time-challenged is to live in the now—the immediate present. They are not known for planning ahead. In fact, they may never have seriously sat down and imagined a picture of what their life might someday be like. This is especially true for adolescent and young adult clients.

This unit provides an opportunity for participants to pause and dream about what they would like to have happen in their lives. They literally draw their future and then, using Planning Ahead by Planning Backwards, they discover a strategy to begin making those dreams happen, right now, by planning the time to start on a step toward making their dreams a reality. It can be a very powerful experience.

Years ago when I asked Dr. Arwood how I was supposed to figure out my future, she responded, "Just draw it." What she understood was the power of a picture for the visual thinker. Seeing yourself, with your dream, on paper, somehow makes it concrete and real. It is no longer floating in your mind. It is visible and now possible. You can then draw the steps that lead to action. This book in your hands was once just a dream drawn on a piece of paper.

This unit also wraps up the course. Beyond addressing future goals, it promotes discussion about the choices we make minute-by-minute in our lives. It provides information about how to be realistic about the process of behavior change. It also contains a second self-assessment for participants to pause and note their behavior changes since the beginning of the course and to appraise the areas that still need improvement.

Topics in this unit include:

- Planning your future
- Changing behavior
- Being resilient
- Second self-assessment
- The power of choice

MATERIALS NEEDED:

- Self-Assessment Comparison form (from the appendix), one for each participant
- Dry erase board, markers, and eraser
- For each participant (parents included) a copy of the *Seeing My Time* workbook
- Sharp pencils with erasers
- 3 x 5 cards

The Third Truth of Time:

The Way You Use Your Time Equals Your Life

A TV Story

I tell my clients that I won a 45" HD flat screen TV in a raffle. I explain that I burst out laughing when I found out because I almost never watch TV! It's been years since I've turned one on to watch a regular program. I don't have time for it. I've told my husband that when I'm so old that I can't do anything else, then I'll watch the reruns of series I missed and movies I never saw. Until then I'm busy happily making my dreams happen.

Page 47:
The Way You Use Your Time Equals Your Life

So far we have had two Truths of Time: 1) Out of Sight, Out of Mind, and 2) Time Takes Up Space. Now we have the Third Truth of Time: The Way You Use Your Time Equals Your Life.

While we often don't have a lot of choice over our assigned time, at work and school, we do have a choice over how we spend our free time. We can walk in the door at home and jump right on the L-Train and veg out for hours. It is a choice. The other choice is to stay engaged and pursue passions and dreams, to get on the E-Train. We only get so much time on this planet.

This page is about seeing the big picture of our life. It is really about our mortality, though I don't frame it that way for my clients. Instead, I open up a brief discussion about choices and values and purpose.

The prompt in this section can perplex some adolescents who are trying to wrap their brain around such an expanse of time. However, it sets their metacognition in motion. I had a fourteen-year-old male ADHD client who was uninterested in school. In fact, he had no area of discernible interest beyond his girlfriend. He drew a complete blank when asked to draw his future, but his key idea for the session was: "I need to figure out what I want to do."

WHAT I DO:

Direct participants to page 47.

ACTIVITY:

1. **Ask** a participant to read the heading and subheading on the page: *The Third Truth of Time: The Way You Use Your Time Equals Your Life.*

2. **Say:** All the little choices we make about how we act and how we use our time end up equaling the story of our life. We have so many choices.

   - What kind of life do you want to have?
   - Do you want adventures?
   - Do you want challenges?

- Do you want to be remembered for helping people?
- Do you want to create something or accomplish a specific goal?
- Do you want a quiet life with family and friends and good food?

3. **Direct** participants to answer the prompt: *How do you want to remember your life?* **Share** responses.

Seeing My Future

First, draw yourself in the middle and then draw what you would like to do in the future.

Page 48:
Seeing My Future

For the time-challenged visual thinker, the future is an amorphous concept. It isn't real or concrete. Drawing the future is a way to connect our present actions with future goals and dreams.

A Story of a Failure

Having a student draw their future can be really powerful. At least three times, that I know of, it has transformed the lives of struggling young people. One was an eighth-grader brought to me by his grandmother, a teacher I respected a great deal. He was a bright kid, but he was skipping school and not doing his work. His family life had major challenges.

He lived almost two hours away from me, so I spent ninety minutes with him, giving my all to get him to come back to complete the course. At the end of that time, he told me he wasn't interested in coming back. I was so disappointed.

Years later, I saw his grandmother. She greeted me and told me that I had saved her grandson's life. "What?" I wondered. "Why did she say that?" This guy was one of my failures.

She told me that he hung in there and went to school regularly—getting mostly Cs. When he graduated, the family scraped money together and bought him a state-of-the-art 35mm camera. When I talked with his grandmother, he was enrolled in a prestigious photojournalism program and doing very well.

In reflecting back over my session with him, I remembered I'd had him draw his future and had talked about how school and living at home were only going to be a few more years and then he'd be able to pursue his own dreams. He just had to get though the system. I believe that by seeing his life beyond the school he didn't enjoy and his difficult home life, he was able to hang in there to graduate.

WHAT I DO:

1. **Direct** participants to page 48.

2. **Say:** Just as we can draw what we want and need to do in a week, we can draw our future. On this page you are encouraged to dream big.

Ask: What do you want do in your lifetime?
- Travel?
- Go to college?
- Make lots of money?
- Help people?
- Have a family?
- Be famous?
- Create something?
- Write a book?
- Make a movie?
- Learn a skill?

ACTIVITY:

1. **Direct** participants to draw their long-term future goals on page 48. Have them first draw a picture of themselves in the center and then draw little symbols for different dreams.

2. **Explain** that they are going to have a few quiet minutes to work on this.

   NOTE: For the instructor, this is the hardest part of teaching this course. You have to sit and be quiet for a few minutes. Let them get a good start on a number of goals before moving them on.

3. **Ask** each participant to explain their drawing.

4. **Say:** This activity can be done at least once a year because our dreams get revised as we reach our goals.

Tip

I draw my future every January 1st. I sit down in the quiet morning with a cup of tea and draw. I put down both long-term and short-term goals. It is pretty amazing to look back and see what I have accomplished with this kind of forward planning.

Page 49:
Three Months of Goals

This page begins bringing future plans into the present in a version of Planning Ahead by Planning Backwards.

WHAT I DO:

1. **Direct** participants to page 49.

2. **Say:** On this page you are going to connect to those distant future goals and start to make some of them happen.

ACTIVITY:

1. **Direct** participants to draw on page 49.

2. **Explain** that as in the last activity, they should draw themselves in the middle of the box on page 49.

3. **Direct** participants to look back to page 48 and do the following:

    - Choose three or four of those future goals to draw on this page.

    - Under each goal symbol, write a couple of steps you could take in the next three months that would get you closer to your goals.

4. **Allow** participants a couple of minutes to work on this.

5. **Briefly** allow participants to share the steps they are going to take in the next three months to get closer to a dream or future goal.

Page 50:
My Week of Actions

This page brings the future into the present by putting a specific action into plans for the coming week. There isn't time in the session for participants to detail all their plans for the week, so they should be encouraged to continue this process at home.

WHAT I DO:

1. **Direct** participants to page 50.

2. **Say:** On this page you are going to connect the goals for the next three months to the goals for the coming week. You are actually going to begin doing actions that will help you reach your dreams.

ACTIVITY:

1. **Direct** participants to once again draw themselves in the middle of the box on page 50. Have them draw one or two future goals.

   List exactly what action or step they will take this week to begin reaching their dreams.

2. **Ask** them to estimate how much time their action is going to take and write it down in time circles.

3. **Explain** that they will only be able to plan to work on a couple of goals for this coming week. They should finish the process of planning their week at home.

4. **Briefly** allow participants to share the steps they are going to take in the next week to get closer to their future goal.

5. **Point out** that the strategy they just completed is another example of Planning Ahead by Planning Backwards. They started in the future and began breaking the big dream into steps.

Page 51:
Summary for Reaching Goals

The time-challenged need visual reminders to plan for their future. They need a picture of the future to begin the process of breaking long-term goals and dreams into steps. It is the process that follows the concept of Planning Ahead by Planning Backwards, which was also used to get projects done by a deadline.

This page provides a visual summary of the strategy used to focus on the future while still in the present. It is a step-by-step procedure. Picture the destination and then figure out the steps needed to get there.

WHAT I DO:

1. **Direct** participants to page 51.

2. **Explain** that it is a visual summary of the steps they just went through as they planned how to begin working on future goals.

   It shows how to look far ahead and then break those dreams into steps that can be done in three months, then this week, and finally done today.

3. **Explain** that this page is for future reference to be used after the course is over.

   It is recommended to pick a day, like the first of January, your birthday, or the first day of school, to sit down and appraise your life goals and dreams. Draw them and then make a three-month plan.

   Refer back to that three-month plan when you are doing your weekly planning. When three months are up, go back to the big picture and make a new three-month plan.

   Keep updating your three-month plan and evaluate your progress, until a year passes. It is very gratifying to see progress on dreams.

Page 52:
Changing My Behavior

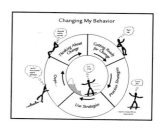

If you ask the typical person how long it takes to change a significant behavior and create a new habit, they will often say, "Twenty-one days," or "One month." If only it were that quick and easy. Researchers Prochaska and DiClemente investigated how people change as applied to addictive behaviors. Their answer on how long it takes to let go of one ingrained behavior and to substitute positive behaviors: three to five years.

It is critical for participants in this course to have realistic expectations for their behavior changes. They were told in the first session that there is no magic wand to fix a brain with executive functioning challenges. If your clients are adolescents, they've already learned that they can't expect to have an adult functioning brain until around twenty-five years of age. That fact alone confirms that it is going to take years for them to develop fully independent time-management skills.

Being realistic doesn't mean that behavior change can't happen. It can. Over the seven sessions, your clients have observed themselves making changes and have experienced the benefits of those changes. It happens one decision at a time, one choice at a time.

Prochaska and DiClemente describe the change process as being circular, beginning at a point where an individual first decides he wants to make a change and begins the process by getting help. After getting help comes practicing the new behavior. With practice an individual can feel fixed. Yet when faced with major stress or transition, he may slip back into old negative behavior. The solution is to think of the process as cyclical. One can always choose again to change. Getting back to good behavior takes less time as you go through the experience of slipping and then recommitting to change.

Page 52 is a visual of the circular process of changing behavior.

WHAT I DO:

1. **Direct** participants to page 52.

2. **Provide** the following explanation for the graphic:

Key Points

1. Changing a behavior, like creating excellent time-management skills, can take years.

2. Be patient with yourself and those around you as you work on changing behaviors.

3. Getting back to good behavior takes less time as you go through the experience of slipping and then recommitting to change.

4. Little by little, change happens.

- This course has been about changing behavior, specifically time-management behavior.

- You started like the figure on the top left, wondering if your life couldn't be more fun, less stressful, and more successful (with fewer people frustrated and angry with you).

- You were thinking about change (or your parent was thinking about change), so you moved around to the figure on the top right. This is where you met me. You had the courage to get help.

- Since we've been working through the course, you have been practicing the strategies that compensate for the executive functioning skills your brain doesn't have. You are like the figure on the bottom right just learning to skateboard.

- Over time you'll become very good at using these strategies. You'll be on the E-Train. You'll be coasting like the figure in the middle of the circle.

- And then, do you see that mountain inside the circle? That stands for "life happens." You'll be skating along and crash! Something upsets your pattern: you get sick, somebody in your family gets sick, you have to move. Under pressure you decide you don't have time to plan your week or your day, much less your future, so you stop supporting your brain with these external tools you've learned to use.

- What happens? Life gets worse! More stressful! You'll be like the figure who fell off the skateboard and is hanging on for dear life, trying to figure out what to do next.

- That's the time to get this book out again. Sit down with it for just a few minutes to review, as we've done at the beginning of each session.

- It'll remind you about what you need to do to support your brain so you can get back on the E-Train of time management.

ACTIVITY:

1. **Say:** There is research on how long it takes for a behavior change to become automatic. How long do you think it takes to create a new habit, one that is so natural you no longer have to think about it, you just do it? (Share guesses.)

2. **Say:** The answer, based on research working with folks with alcohol and drug addictions, is . . . three to five years. Yes, that is years.

3. **Say:** We don't make major behavior changes overnight, or even in twenty-one days or in three months. It takes years of metacognition, of consciously choosing to use support strategies, to develop great time-management skills.

4. **Say:** The good news is that you have just begun a wonderful journey. With this course and this book, you now have the knowledge, skills, and strategies that can change your life so you can reach your full potential by using external strategies to support your brain.

5. **Emphasize:** Be patient with yourself (and with each other). Little by little, you can do it.

A Story About Behavior Change

I found the information about how long it takes to make behavior changes when I was taking a weight-loss class, in which the behavior change was connected to eating.

I proved it to be true when it came to developing an exercising habit. It took three years of talking myself out of bed to get to the gym or yoga studio at 6:30 in the morning. "It's raining. I'm still tired . . . No. Get up. Get dressed. Get moving." Now it is an automatic habit. I don't like it when I can't exercise for some reason. And I've kept off that thirty pounds now for many years!

Page 53:
Life Can Be Rough—
You Gotta Be Tough

Our culture today goes out of its way to cushion our children from pain, failure, or struggle. Many of us, including Stanford researcher Carol Dweck, author of *Mindset: The New Psychology of Success*, worry that we are raising children who lack the resilience to bounce back and start over when life doesn't go according to plan.

The purpose of this page is to acknowledge that we don't always get what we want when we want it. Life can throw some pretty tough curves our way. Successful people don't fear failure. They see challenges as learning opportunities. They persevere.

WHAT I DO:

1. **Direct** participants to page 53.

2. **Say:** Life isn't always kind. We can have great plans that get changed by events outside our control.

3. **Explain:** One important trait of successful people is that they don't give up. They may get flattened or spun around, but they follow the old advice: "Pick yourself up, dust yourself off, and start all over again."

ACTIVITY:

1. **Direct** participants to respond to the words: *Life can be rough—you gotta be tough.*

2. **Ask** them to write or draw what the words mean for them. **Share** responses.

Pages 54–55:
Second Self-Assessments

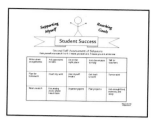

The second self-assessment allows participants to pause and reflect back over their behavior changes. Just as they did with the first self-assessment, they will rate themselves on a scale of 0 to 5. Remember, the score isn't as important as the metacognitive process of self-assessment.

After participants fill out their second self-assessment, you will provide them with the scores from their first self-assessment to allow them to see their progress and to acknowledge the areas that still need attention. Sometimes the score given this time is lower than the first self-assessment. I've had clients admit that they padded their first scores and that the present score is a more accurate representation of their behavior.

MATERIALS NEEDED:

In advance of the session, complete the Self-Assessment Comparison form for each participant by filling in the responses from their first self-assessment. This form is in the appendix. (If you did not complete this form during session one, you'll have to look at each participant's *Course Notes* to get their scores.)

WHAT I DO:

1. **Direct** adolescent participants to page 54 and adult participants to page 55.

2. **Explain** that the course is just about complete, so it is time, once again, to do a self-assessment of their behavior.

   Say: Rate yourself on a scale of 0 to 5. Zero means you never do it. Five means you do it all the time.

   Circle your scores. (The circled score will shortly be compared with their score from their first self-assessment.)

3. **Once** the participants have filled in their new scores, **read** them their first scores, which you filled in on the Self-Assessment Comparison form during the first session. Have them record the old scores in the coordinating boxes next to their new circled scores.

Key Points

1. Participants will have experienced improvement in some of the areas.

2. It is OK to still have room for improvement. Little by little …

170

- Compare scores, noting improvements and areas that still need attention. Acknowledge the successes. If you have time, do some problem solving about the areas that need some focus.

- Remind them of the saying, "Little by little, change happens." This course lasts only a few hours. They have just begun to make changes that will impact the rest of their lives.

Page 56:
Plan Your Work—Work Your Plan

My husband often tells tales of his autocratic high school headmaster. Among other things, he would sit before the boys of his school and admonish them to: "Plan your work. Then work your plan." As an educator, I don't approve of many things that old-style headmaster did, but he was absolutely correct about the need to plan your work and then follow the plan with action.

As this course winds down to its final minutes, you need to admonish your clients to plan the time to plan. If they don't, then the whole course has been a waste of time and money.

WHAT I DO:

1. **Direct** participants to page 56.

2. **Explain:**

   • During this course, you have begun developing the necessary metacognition—a conscious voice in your head—that connects you to the passage of time and your behavior.

   • This is a critical part of developing the executive functioning skill of time management.

   • However, all the time and money you put into this course will amount to nothing if you don't take the time to sit down and plan out your weeks and your days. So...

ACTIVITY:

Direct participants to answer the prompt: *When am I going to do my planning?* **Share** responses.

Key Point
The best way to successfully manage time is to schedule the time to plan your week, and then to plan each day.

Check In - Check Out

Self Reflections

The check in and check out self-reflection pages build in pauses for participants to access and improve their metacognitive capacity. These pauses are critical to help them change their behavior. It gives you a chance to stop talking so they can think.

As I ask each participant for his or her responses, everyone gets a window into that person's thinking. It sheds light into an otherwise private area, which can improve communication and understanding between participants. It is also an opportunity for genuine acknowledgment of their improving metacognition, their thinking about they thinking, the primary reason the Sklar Process is effective as a way to improve time management and organization.

Page 66:
Self-Reflection
Session #1 Check Out

MATERIALS NEEDED:

- 3 x 5 index card (Key Card) to write the key idea and homework assignment

CHECK OUT ACTIVITIES:

1. **Direct** participants to the left side of page 66, Session #1 Check Out.

2. **Direct** participants to write or draw their key idea from today's session. The key idea represents one idea or concept that the participant specifically wants to remember.

3. **Share** responses, going around the table, allowing each participant to name their key idea.

4. **Give** participants the following assignment:

   - Time one activity that you like to do.

   - Time one task or activity that you don't like to do.

   Suggest they time mundane tasks like emptying the dishwasher as well as fun ones like time spent on Facebook or email.

5. **Tell** them they will report back on their timing of activities at the beginning of the next session.

6. **Tell** them to write the assignment on page 66.

7. **Give** them a Key Card to take home as a reminder. Have them write their key idea for the day as well as their homework assignment.

END OF SESSION

NOTE: In the appendix there is a Session Record Form used for planning sessions and to record the progress made during each session. Use it to record material covered, personal observations and notes needed to begin the next session.

Print off at least six of these forms so you'll be ready for future sessions.

Page 66:
Self-Reflection
Session #2 Check In

REVIEW:

Tell participants that at the beginning of each of the remaining sessions, you will be asking them to take a couple of minutes to review—scan—their *Course Notes* from the beginning of the book through to the end of the most recent session.

Ask them to let you know if something is unclear or confusing from the most recent session so that you can provide clarification. (This should take a maximum of two minutes.)

SELF-REFLECTION:

1. **Direct** participants to page 66.

2. **Explain** that a primary goal of the course is to develop conscious metacognition connected to time. The two check-in questions on page 66 focus on developing metacognition.

3. **Ask** participants to reflect back on the activities they chose to time during the past week: something they didn't like to do and something they did like to do.

4. **Ask** them to write their answer to the first question on page 66. (If they didn't remember to do the assignment, have them put down *Didn't do it*. Just acknowledge that you are pleased to have an honest answer and leave it at that.)

5. **Ask** them to reflect back over the last week and see if they made any changes in behavior because of what they learned in the first session.

6. **Ask** them to write their answer to the second question on page 66. (If they didn't make any changes, have them write *No changes*.)

7. **Let** each participant read their answers and discuss them as needed. Celebrate changes. Don't spend too much time here.

Tip

It is important to be accepting of participants who didn't do the homework assignment. It is early in the course, and developing metacognition and behavior change takes time and patience.

Page 67:
Self-Reflection
Session #2 Check Out

MATERIALS NEEDED:

- 3 x 5 Key Card to write the key idea and homework assignment

CHECK OUT ACTIVITIES:

1. **Direct** participants to the left side of page 67, Session #2 Check Out.

2. **Direct** participants to write or draw their key idea from to-day's session.

3. **Give** the following assignment:
   - Students should time how long it takes to actually do a typical homework assignment, such as math or English.

   - Adults should time how long it takes to do typical tasks like grocery shopping, menu planning, or specific housecleaning chores.

4. **Ask** them to write their assignment on page 67 and on a Key Card to take home as a reminder.

END OF SESSION

NOTE: On the Session Record Form (In the appendix) record material covered during the session, as well as observations and planning for the next session.

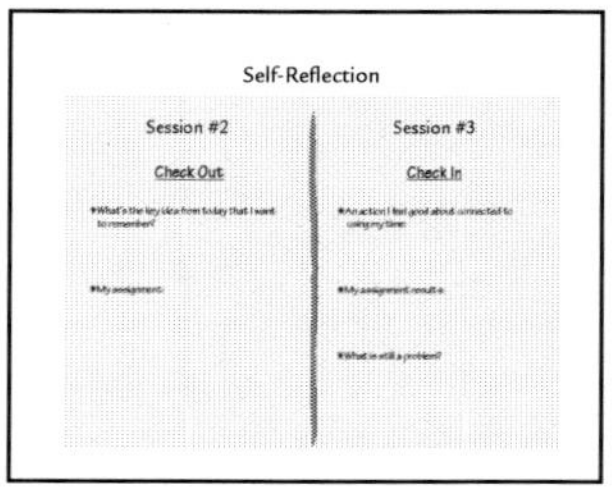

Page 67:
Self-Reflection
Session #3 Check In

WHAT I DO:

Tell participants to take a couple of minutes to review their *Course Notes* from the beginning of the book through to the end of the most recent session. **Encourage** them to ask for clarification if needed.

ACTIVITY:

1. **Direct** participants to the right side of page 67 and have them complete the three prompts.

2. **Tell** each participant to read their answers and discuss them as needed. Be encouraging and remind them that change happens little by little. They have just begun.

    It is important to be accepting of participants who didn't do the homework assignment. Thank them for giving you an honest answer. It is early in the course, and developing metacognition and behavior change takes time and patience.

Page 68:
Self-Reflection
Session #3 Check Out

MATERIALS NEEDED:

- 3 x 5 Key Card to write the key idea and homework assignment

CHECK OUT ACTIVITIES:

1. **Direct** everyone to write or draw their key idea from today's session on page 68.

2. **Ask** them to write a Time Tool they would like to try, for example using a timer for taking breaks or using a dry erase board for the whole family's plans. (They can put down more than one if they like.)

3. **Give** participants the assignment to get the time tools of their choice.

4. **Direct** participants to write their assignment on page 68 and on a Key Card to take home as a reminder.

END OF SESSION

NOTE: On the Session Record Form (from the appendix) record material covered during the session, as well as observations and planning for the next session.

Page 68:
Self-Reflection
Session #4 Check In

WHAT I DO:

Tell participants to take a couple of minutes to review their *Course Notes* from the beginning of the book through to the end of the most recent session. **Encourage** them to ask for clarification if needed.

ACTIVITY:

1. **Direct** participants to page 68 and have them answer the three prompts on the right.

2. **Direct** participants to read their answers and discuss them as needed. Praise them for what is working well. This is often an opportunity to help families and individuals do some problem solving around the third prompt: What could work better?

Page 69:
Self-Reflection
Session #4 Check Out

MATERIALS NEEDED:

- 3 x 5 Key Card to write the key idea and homework assignment

CHECK OUT ACTIVITIES:

1. **Direct** participants to write or draw their key idea from to-day's session.

2. **Ask** them to write one or more strategies they would like to try. Options include:

   - Drawing their assignment

   - Using sticky notes to break a large task into steps

   - Planning ahead by planning backwards

   - Using sticky notes on a Month Calendar for planning

   - Drawing time circles when they are estimating the time needed to complete a project

3. **Give** participants the opportunity to choose their own assignment for the week. What do they need to do this week that will improve their time management? (For example, they might choose to plan a project using the Planning-Ahead-by-Planning-Backwards strategy, or they might decide to use a timer to begin working on an overwhelming project like cleaning a messy closet.)

4. **Direct** participants to write their assignment on page 69 and on a Key Card to take home as a reminder.

5. **Direct** participants to share their responses to the prompts on page 69.

6. **Inform** participants that the next session will cover organization and paper management.

• Students should bring binders, backpacks, and planners.

• Adults may bring their planners and a small pile of papers they need to go through.

Just prior to the next session, it is a good idea to send a reminder email to participants to bring these items.

END OF SESSION

NOTE: On the Session Record Form (from the appendix), record material covered during the session, as well as observations and planning for the next session.

Page 69:
Self-Reflection
Session #5 Check In

This check in has an added element of timing how long it takes the participants to do their review of the workbook. The purpose of timing this activity is to provide a concrete experience of how long it actually takes to do a review of material. This is especially important for students because you will now define this review activity as "studying."

Adolescents often confuse the words *homework* and *studying*, thinking of them as synonymous. They are not. Homework is just school work done outside of school. To study something means you are devoting time to learning, to reviewing content, not just turning in an assignment. (Honestly, how many turned-in assignments do you recall?) Remember, it is with repeated exposure to material that we build the neuron connections in the brain required to actually learn something.

It is a novel idea to many students to review material for the sake of learning it. It is important to point out that if they just spent a few minutes each evening reviewing, say, their Spanish vocabulary words, they would not only get better grades on quizzes and tests, they might actually learn Spanish!

MATERIALS NEEDED:

- A timer with a count-up function

WHAT I DO:

1. **Tell** participants to take a couple of minutes to review their workbook from the beginning of the book through to the end of the most recent session. Encourage them to ask for clarification if needed. Begin timing the review without telling the participants.

2. Once they have completed the review, **ask** each participant to guess how long it took for them to review the material. Answers will vary. The time-challenged are notorious for poorly estimating how long they've been working at a task. Tell participants that you had timed their review and tell them the amount of time it took.

3. **Say**: The reason we review at the beginning of each session is to build neuron connections in your brain so that you can learn and remember the material. In essence, you have been studying. You are remembering what we've covered and getting ready to connect new information to old information in your brain. You are literally strengthening your neuron connections by reviewing.

ACTIVITY:

1. **Direct** participants to page 69 and have them answer the three prompts.

2. **Ask** each participant read their answers and discuss them as needed.

Page 70:
Self-Reflection
Session #5 Check Out

MATERIALS NEEDED:

• 3 x 5 Key Card to write the key idea and homework assignment

CHECK OUT ACTIVITIES:

1. **Direct** participants to write or draw their key idea from today's session on page 70.

2. **Ask** them to write one or more strategies they would like to try. Options include:

    • Designate homes for belongings that are often misplaced.
    • Use a timer for five- to fifteen-minute cleaning sprees to begin getting rid of piles.
    • Use an inbox and outbox folder in a school binder.
    • Plan five minutes to go through the papers in the inbox.
    • Organize a personal binder or planner.
    • Get an external hard drive for the computer or a backup system on a website.
    • Email homework assignments to teachers.
    • Review notes or preview material before class or meetings.
    • Turn off distractions while working on homework or desk work.

3. **Give** participants the opportunity to choose their own assignment for the week. What do they need to do this week that will improve their time management?

4. **Ask** participants to share their responses to the prompts on page 70.

5. **Direct** participants to write their assignment on page 46 and on a Key Card to take home as a reminder.

END OF SESSION

NOTE: On the Session Record Form (from the appendix) record material covered during the session, as well as observations and planning for the next session.

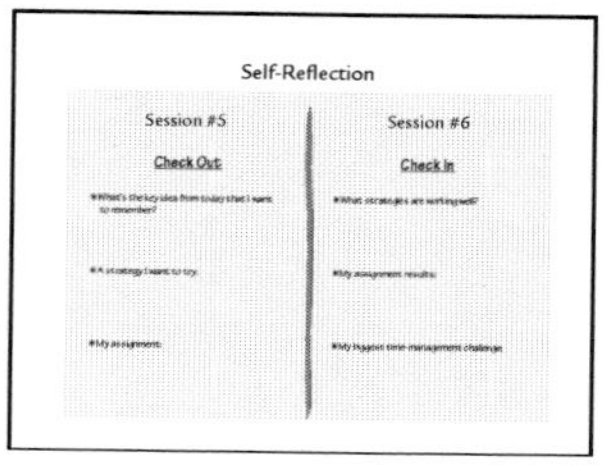

Page 70:
Self-Reflection
Session #6 Check In

WHAT I DO:

Tell participants to take a couple of minutes to review their *Course Notes* from the beginning of the book through to the end of the most recent session. **Encourage** them to ask for clarification if needed.

ACTIVITY:

1. **Direct** participants to page 70 and have them answer the three prompts.

2. **Ask** participants to read their answers and discuss them as needed. Praise them for what is working well.

   This is an opportunity to help families and individuals do some problem solving around the third prompt: *My biggest time-management challenge.*

   Remind them of the words that began the course: *Little by little, change happens.*

Page 71:
Self-Reflection
Session #6 Check Out

MATERIALS NEEDED:

• 3 x 5 Key Card to write the key idea and homework assignment

NOTE: If you have finished the course materials in six sessions, you will not need to send home a Key Card because the participants will be taking home their *Seeing My Time* workbook.

CHECK OUT ACTIVITIES:

1. Direct participants to write or draw their key idea from today's session on page 71.

2. **Ask** them to write a strategy that they want to get better at using.

3. **Ask** them what they could do to manage their life for less stress?

4. **Share** their responses.

Page 71:
Self-Reflection
Session #7 Check In

ACTIVITY:

1. **Direct** participants to page 71 and have them answer the three prompts.

2. **Ask** participants to read their answers and discuss them as needed. Praise them for what is working well.

Page 72:
Self-Reflection
Session #7 Check Out

MATERIALS NEEDED:

• 3 x 5 Key Card to write the key idea and homework assignment

NOTE: If you have finished the course materials in seven sessions, you will not need to send home a Key Card because the participants will be taking home their *Seeing My Time* workbook.

CHECK OUT ACTIVITIES:

1. Direct participants to write or draw their key idea from today's session on page 72.

2. **Ask** them what strategy they want to get better at using.

3. **Ask** them to create their own assignment stating what could they do to make their life work better.

4. **Share** their responses.

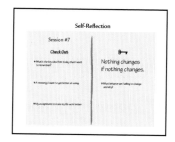

Page 72:

Nothing Changes if Nothing Changes

I can't remember where I first picked up these words: *Nothing changes if nothing changes*. I just know that there was a time when I needed them, and I put them in a prominent place on the refrigerator to inspire myself to be conscious of my power, my ability to choose how I move through my life, through my day, through my minutes.

I tell my clients that we can be victims of circumstance, of our biology—our genetic makeup—or we can choose to make changes and improve our life. The time-challenged, those with executive functioning deficits and perhaps learning differences too, can choose to live a limited life with those innate restrictions. Or they can choose to use strategies and tools that get them around those limitations. They can ask for help when they need it.

Time is precious. Life is precious. It is fleeting. If you are unsatisfied with how your life is going, then have the courage to make a change.

Little by little, change happens.

WHAT I DO:

Direct participants to the right side of page 72.

ACTIVITY:

1. **Ask** a participant to read aloud the final words in the course: *Nothing changes if nothing changes.*

2. **Say:**

• At this point, you now have the metacognition required to manage your time.

• You have external strategies to support your brain so you can get things done.

• You've thought about when you are going to do your planning.

Key Points

1. Armed with the information and tools from this course, it is now a personal decision—a choice—to manage your time.

2. You can no longer blame anyone else—or even your brain.

- The final step? It comes down to that pause point of choosing, that moment of stopping for a moment to think about what is the best choice for using your next bit of time. How we use our time is our choice. Our choices make up our life.

- Your choice now is to choose, or not, to use the strategies you've learned in this course. It's up to you. You have the tools in your workbook, but if you don't choose to use them, you are going to continue to struggle to reach your goals, and the people around you are going to be frustrated with you.

- Nothing changes if nothing changes.

3. **Direct** participants to answer the final prompt: *What behavior am I willing to change and why?*

4. **Ask:** What behavior is stopping them from reaching their full potential?

5. **Share** responses and leave them with the encouraging words: *Little by little, change happens.* They can do it!

END OF SESSION

On the Session Record Form (from the appendix), record material covered during the session, as well as observations and planning for the next session, if needed.

NOTE: If your clients require eight to nine sessions to complete the course material, then you will have them check in and check out beginning on page 73 of the workbook.

Pages 73-74:
Self-Reflection
Sessions #8 and #9 Check In

NOTE: It is only necessary to use these pages if your client requires eight to nine sessions to complete the course.

WHAT I DO:

Tell participants to take a couple of minutes to review their workbook from the beginning of the book through to the end of the most recent session. **Encourage** them to ask for clarification if needed.

ACTIVITY:

1. **Direct** participants to the appropriate pages and have them answer the three prompts.

2. **Ask** each participant to read their answers and discuss them as needed. Praise them for what is working well.

3. **Remind** them of the words that began the course: *Little by little, change happens.*

Pages 73-74:
Self-Reflection
Sessions #8 and #9 Check Out

CHECK OUT ACTIVITIES:

1. **Direct** participants to write or draw their key idea from today's session on the appropriate page.

2. **Ask** them to write a strategy that they want to get better at using.

3. **Ask** them to give themselves an assignment to enable them to manage their time to reduce stress.

4. **Share** their responses.

Appendix

Session Record Form
Seeing My Time

Client(s) Attending: _____

Date: _____ Session # _____ Payment Status: _____

Course Notes pages and topics covered:

Observations:

Planning for next session:

Follow-up:

Adult Self-Assessment Comparison

Client Name: _____ Date: _____

Skill	Self-Assessment #1	Self-Assessment #2
Use a Calendar		
Use a Planner		
Plan My Week		
See My Day		
Digital Timers		
See the Time		
Analog Clocks		
Handle Paper		
Tickler File		
File Papers		
Create Space		
Restorative Time		
Eat Well		
Exercise		
Sleep		

Student Self-Assessment Comparison

Client Name: _____ Date: _____

Skill	Self-Assessment #1	Self-Assessment #2
Write down assignments		
Ask questions in class		
Sit in the right place		
Ask classmates for help		
Talk to teachers		
Plan for homework		
Start my work		
Give myself breaks		
Get back to work		
Turn in work		
Wear a watch		
Use analog clocks where I need them		
Organize papers		
Plan projects		
Get enough food, exercise, and sleep		

My Week of Actions!

Dates _____

Monday	Tuesday	Wednesday	Thursday	Friday	Saturday	Sunday
Date	Date	Date	Date	Date	Date	Date
6:00	6:00	6:00	6:00	6:00	6:00	6:00
6:30	6:30	6:30	6:30	6:30	6:30	6:30
7:00	7:00	7:00	7:00	7:00	7:00	7:00
7:30	7:30	7:30	7:30	7:30	7:30	7:30
8:00	8:00	8:00	8:00	8:00	8:00	8:00
8:30	8:30	8:30	8:30	8:30	8:30	8:30
9:00	9:00	9:00	9:00	9:00	9:00	9:00
9:30	9:30	9:30	9:30	9:30	9:30	9:30
10:00	10:00	10:00	10:00	10:00	10:00	10:00
10:30	10:30	10:30	10:30	10:30	10:30	10:30
11:00	11:00	11:00	11:00	11:00	11:00	11:00
11:30	11:30	11:30	11:30	11:30	11:30	11:30
12:00	12:00	12:00	12:00	12:00	12:00	12:00
12:30	12:30	12:30	12:30	12:30	12:30	12:30
1:00	1:00	1:00	1:00	1:00	1:00	1:00
1:30	1:30	1:30	1:30	1:30	1:30	1:30
2:00	2:00	2:00	2:00	2:00	2:00	2:00
2:30	2:30	2:30	2:30	2:30	2:30	2:30
3:00	3:00	3:00	3:00	3:00	3:00	3:00
3:30	3:30	3:30	3:30	3:30	3:30	3:30
4:00	4:00	4:00	4:00	4:00	4:00	4:00
4:30	4:30	4:30	4:30	4:30	4:30	4:30
5:00	5:00	5:00	5:00	5:00	5:00	5:00
5:30	5:30	5:30	5:30	5:30	5:30	5:30
6:00	6:00	6:00	6:00	6:00	6:00	6:00
6:30	6:30	6:30	6:30	6:30	6:30	6:30
7:00	7:00	7:00	7:00	7:00	7:00	7:00
7:30	7:30	7:30	7:30	7:30	7:30	7:30
8:00	8:00	8:00	8:00	8:00	8:00	8:00
8:30	8:30	8:30	8:30	8:30	8:30	8:30
9:00	9:00	9:00	9:00	9:00	9:00	9:00
9:30	9:30	9:30	9:30	9:30	9:30	9:30
10:00	10:00	10:00	10:00	10:00	10:00	10:00
10:30	10:30	10:30	10:30	10:30	10:30	10:30
11:00	11:00	11:00	11:00	11:00	11:00	11:00

Monday	Tuesday	Wednesday	Thursday	Friday	Saturday	Sunday
2:30	2:30	2:30	2:30	2:30	2:30	2:30
3:00	3:00	3:00	3:00	3:00	3:00	3:00
3:30	3:30	3:30	3:30	3:30	3:30	3:30
4:00	4:00	4:00	4:00	4:00	4:00	4:00
4:30	4:30	4:30	4:30	4:30	4:30	4:30
5:00	5:00	5:00	5:00	5:00	5:00	5:00
5:30	5:30	5:30	5:30	5:30	5:30	5:30
6:00	6:00	6:00	6:00	6:00	6:00	6:00
6:30	6:30	6:30	6:30	6:30	6:30	6:30
7:00	7:00	7:00	7:00	7:00	7:00	7:00
7:30	7:30	7:30	7:30	7:30	7:30	7:30
8:00	8:00	8:00	8:00	8:00	8:00	8:00
8:30	8:30	8:30	8:30	8:30	8:30	8:30
9:00	9:00	9:00	9:00	9:00	9:00	9:00
9:30	9:30	9:30	9:30	9:30	9:30	9:30
10:00	10:00	10:00	10:00	10:00	10:00	10:00
10:30	10:30	10:30	10:30	10:30	10:30	10:30
11:00	11:00	11:00	11:00	11:00	11:00	11:00
Date	Date	Date	Date	Date	Date	Date

My Day

6:00 _____
6:30 _____
7:00 _____
7:30 _____
8:00 _____
8:30 _____
9:00 _____
9:30 _____
10:00 _____
10:30 _____
11:00 _____
11:30 _____
12:00 _____
12:30 _____
1:00 _____
1:30 _____
2:00 _____
2:30 _____
3:00 _____
3:30 _____
4:00 _____
4:30 _____
5:00 _____
5:30 _____
6:00 _____
6:30 _____
7:00 _____
7:30 _____
8:00 _____
8:30 _____
9:00 _____
9:30 _____
10:00 _____
10:30 _____
11:00 _____
11:30 _____

Date _____

Bibliography

Ahern, C. (2009). "Executive Functioning and Learning." Association of Educational Therapists, Bay Area Workshop.

Allen, D. (2001). *Getting Things Done: The Art of Stress-Free Productivity*. New York: Penguin Books.

Barkley, R. (2011) *Barkley Deficits in Executive Functioning Scale (BDEFS for Adults)*. New York: The Guilford Press.

Barkley, R. (2012) *Barkley Deficits in Executive Functioning Scale—Children and Adolescents (BDEFS-CA)*. New York: The Guilford Press.

Barkley, R. (2012). *Executive Functions: What They Are, How They Work, and Why They Evolved*. New York: The Guilford Press.

Barkley, R. (2010). "The Link Between ADHD, Self-Regulation, and Executive Functioning: What it Means for the Treatment of ADHD." Association of Educational Therapists, Annual Conference, Woodland Hills.

Brafman, O., and Brafman, R. (2010). *Click: the Magic of Instant Connections*. New York: Crown Business.

Covey, S. (2004). *The 7 Habits of Highly Effective People: Powerful Lessons in Personal Change*. New York: Free Press.

Dawson, P., and Guare, R. (2009). *Smart but Scattered: The Revolutionary "Executive Skills" Approach to Helping Children Reach Their Potential*. New York: The Guilford Press.

Dawson, P., and Guare, R. (2010). *Executive Skills in Children and Adolescents: A Practical Guide to Assessment and Intervention*, 2nd ed. New York: The Guilford Press.

Dweck, C. (2007). *Mindset: The New Psychology of Success*. New York: Ballantine Books.

Emsellem, H. (2006). *Snooze . . . or Lose! 10 "No-War" Ways to Improve Your Teen's Sleep Habits*. Washington, DC: Joseph Henry Press.

Levine, M. (2002). *A Mind at a Time*. New York: Simon and Schuster.

Margulies, N. (2001). *Mapping Inner Space: Learning and Teaching Visual Mapping*, 2nd ed. Thousand Oaks, CA: Corwin Press.

McGee, T. *How to Become a SuperStar Student*. The Teaching Company.

Medina, J. (2009). *Brain Rules: 12 Principles for Surviving and Thriving at Work, Home, and School*. Seattle: Pear Press.

Meltzer, L. (2010). *Promoting Executive Function in the Classroom*. New York: Guilford Press.

O'Byrne, M. et al. (2005). "Developmental and Emotional Factors in Learning: Mastery and Competence—The Foundations of Self," Association of Educational Therapists, Marin County Area Workshop.

Pink, D. (2006). *A Whole New Mind: Why Right-Brainers Will Rule the Future*. New York: Riverhead Books.

Prochaska, J.O., DiClemente, C.C., and Norcross, J.C. (1992). "In Search of How People Change. Applications to Addictive Behaviors," *The American Psychologist* 47, no. 9, 1102-14.

Roam, D. (2008). *The Back of a Napkin: Solving Problems and Selling Ideas with Pictures*. New York: Portfolio.

Sklar, M. (2010, 2012, 2013). *Seeing My Time: Visual Tools for Executive Functioning Success*. Portland: Aguanga Publishing.

Soderlund, G., Sikstrom, S., and Smart, A. (2007). "Listen to the Noise: Noise Is Beneficial for Cognitive Performance in ADHD," *Journal of Child Psychology and Psychiatry*, 48, no. 8: 840-847.

WEBSITES:

www.ExecutiveFunctioningSuccess.com

Visit Marydee Sklar's website to purchase additional copies of this *Instructor's Manual* as well as the workbook for use by participants: *Seeing My Time: Visual Tools for Executive Functioning Success*. The site also has additional resources, including Cool

Tools, links to timers, and other external tools to support time management. You can sign up for a newsletter. The author welcomes your comments on her blog.

www.teach12.com

The Teaching Company offers a tremendous array of noncredit courses on CD and DVD. I recommend it as a source for students to build background knowledge prior to taking a course for credit.

About the Author

Marydee Sklar is a licensed teacher and a learning coach with a private practice in Portland, Oregon. She specializes in teaching the executive skills of time management and organization to adults as well as adolescents and their parents. She presents to teachers, parents, and professionals on the topic of teaching time-management skills. She has served on the Board of Directors of the Oregon Branch of the International Dyslexia Association and is a general member of the Association of Educational Therapists. Marydee is author of *Seeing My Time: Visual Tools for Executive Functioning Success*, the companion workbook for this instructor's manual. You may contact her through her website:

www.ExecutiveFunctioningSuccess.com.